200 Light
gluten-free recipes

hamlyn | **all color cookbook**

200 Light

gluten-free recipes

An Hachette UK Company
www.hachette.co.uk

First published in Great Britain in 2015 by
Hamlyn, a division of Octopus Publishing Group Ltd
Carmelite House,50 Victoria Embankment,
London EC4Y 0DZ
www.octopusbooks.co.uk

Distributed in the US by Hachette Book Group
1290 Avenue of the Americas, 4th and 5th Floors
New York, NY 10020

Distributed in Canada by Canadian Manda Group
664 Annette St.,Toronto, Ontario, Canada M6S 2C8

Recipes in this book have previously appeared in other books
published by Hamlyn.

ISBN 978-0-600-63224-5

Printed and bound in China

1 2 3 4 5 6 7 8 9 10

Standard level kitchen cup and spoon measurements are used
in all recipes.

Ovens should be preheated to the specific temperature; if using a
convection oven, follow manufacturer's instructions for adjusting the
time and the temperature.

Eggs should be large unless otherwise stated. The U.S. Food and
Drug Administration advises that eggs should not be consumed raw.
This book contains dishes made with raw or lightly cooked eggs. It
is prudent for more vulnerable people, such as pregnant and nursing
mothers, people with weakened immune systems, the elderly, babies,
and young children, to avoid uncooked or lightly cooked dishes made
with eggs. Once prepared, these dishes should be kept refrigerated
and used promptly.

Milk should be whole unless otherwise stated.

Fresh herbs should be used unless otherwise stated.
If unavailable, use dried herbs as an alternative
but use one-third of the quantities stated.

Pepper should be freshly ground black pepper unless
otherwise stated.

This book includes dishes made with nuts and nut derivatives.
It is advisable for customers with known allergic reactions to nuts
and nut derivatives and those who may be potentially vulnerable to
these allergies, such as pregnant and nursing mothers, people with
weakened immune systems, the elderly, babies, and children,
to avoid dishes made with nuts and nut oils. It is also prudent to
check the labels of prepared ingredients for the possible inclusion
of nut derivatives.

contents

introduction

introduction

this series

The Hamlyn All Color Light Series is a collection of books in a handy size, each packed with more than 200 healthy recipes on a variety of topics and cuisines to suit your needs.

The books are designed to help those people who are trying to lose weight by offering a range of delicious recipes that are low in calories but still high in flavor. The recipes show the calorie count per serving, so you will know exactly what you are eating. These are recipes for real and delicious food, not ultra-dieting meals, so they will help you maintain your new, healthier eating plan for life. They must be used as part of a balanced diet, with the cakes and sweet dishes eaten only as an occasional treat.

how to use this book

All the recipes in this book are clearly marked with the number of calories per serving. The chapters cover different calorie bands: less than 500 calories, less than 400 calories, etc.

There are variations of each recipe at the bottom of the page—note the calorie count, because they do vary and can sometimes be more than the original recipe.

The figures assume that you are using reduced or low-fat versions of dairy products, so be sure to use skim milk and low-fat yogurt. They have also been calculated using lean meat, so make sure you trim meat of all

visible fat and remove the skin from chicken breasts. Use moderate amounts of oil and butter for cooking and low-fat/low-calorie alternatives when you can.

Don't forget to take note of the number of servings each recipe makes and divide up the quantity of food accordingly, so that you know exactly how many calories you are consuming. Be careful about side dishes and accompaniments, because they will add to the calorie content.

Above all, enjoy trying out the new flavors and exciting recipes that this book contains. Instead of dwelling on the thought that you are denying yourself your usual unhealthy treats, think of your new diet plan as a positive step toward a new you. Not only will you lose

weight and feel more confident, but your health will benefit, the condition of your hair and nails will improve, and your skin will take on a healthy glow.

the risks of obesity

Up to half of women and two-thirds of men are overweight or obese in the developed world today. Being overweight not only can make us unhappy with our appearance, but can also lead to serious health problems, including heart disease, high blood pressure, and diabetes.

When someone is obese, it means they are overweight to the point that it could start to seriously threaten their health. In fact, obesity ranks as a close second to smoking as a possible cause of cancer. Obese women usually have more complications during and after pregnancy, and people who are overweight or obese are also more at risk of developing coronary heart disease, gallstones, osteoarthritis, high blood pressure, and type-2 diabetes.

how can I tell if I am overweight?

The best way to tell if you are overweight is to work out your body mass index (BMI). To do so, divide your weight in pounds by your height in inches squared and multiply by 703. (For example, if you are 5 feet 6 inches and weigh 146 pounds, the calculation is: 5 x 12 = 60, then 60 + 6 = 66 inches;

66 x 66 = 4,356; 146 ÷ 4,356 = 0.0335; 0.0335 x 703 = 23.56. (Or use an online BMI calculator.) Compare the figure to the list below (the figures should only be applied to healthy adults).

less than 20	underweight
20–25	healthy
25–30	overweight
Over 30	obese

As we all know by now, one of the major causes of obesity is eating too many calories.

what is a calorie?

Our bodies need energy to stay alive, grow, keep warm, and be active. We get the energy we need to survive from the food and beverages we consume—more specifically, from the fat, carbohydrate, protein, and alcohol that they contain.

A calorie (cal), as anyone who has ever been on a diet will know, is the unit used to measure how much energy different foods contain. A calorie can be scientifically defined as the energy required to raise the temperature of 1 gram of water from 58°F to 60°F. A kilocalorie (cal) is 1,000 calories and it is, in fact, kilocalories that we usually mean when we talk about the calories in different foods.

Different food types contain different numbers of calories. For example, a gram of carbohydrate (starch or sugar) provides 3.75 cal, protein provides 4 cal per gram, fat provides 9 cal per gram, and alcohol provides 7 cal per gram. So, fat is the most concentrated source of energy—weight for weight, it provides just over twice as many calories as either protein or carbohydrate—with alcohol not far behind. The energy content of a food or drink depends on how many grams of carbohydrate, fat, protein, and alcohol are present.

how many calories do we need?

The number of calories we need to consume varies from person to person, but your body weight is a clear indication of whether you are eating the right amount. Body weight is simply determined by the number of calories you are eating compared to the number of calories your body is using to maintain itself and needed for physical activity. If you regularly consume more calories than you use, you will start to gain weight, because extra energy is stored in the body as fat.

Based on our relatively inactive modern-day lifestyles, most nutritionists recommend that women should aim to consume about 2,000 calories per day, and men an amount of about 2,500. Of course, the amount of

energy required will depend on your level of activity; the more active you are, the more energy your body will need to maintain a stable weight.

a healthier lifestyle

To maintain a healthy body weight, we need to expend as much energy as we eat; to lose weight, energy expenditure must, therefore, exceed intake of calories. So, exercise is a vital tool in the fight to lose weight. Physical activity doesn't just help us control body weight; it also helps to reduce our appetite and is known to have beneficial effects on the heart and blood that help protect against cardiovascular disease.

Many of us claim we don't enjoy exercise and simply don't have the time to fit it into our hectic schedules, so the easiest way to increase physical activity is by incorporating it into our daily routines, perhaps by walking or cycling instead of driving (particularly for short journeys), getting involved in more active hobbies, such as gardening, and taking small and simple steps, such as using the stairs instead of the elevator whenever possible.

As a general guide, adults should aim to undertake at least 30 minutes of moderate-intensity exercise, such as a brisk walk, five times a week. The 30 minutes does not have to be taken all at once; three sessions of 10 minutes are equally beneficial. Children and young people should be encouraged to get at least 60 minutes of moderate-intensity exercise every day.

Some activities will use up more energy than others. The following list shows some examples of the energy a person weighing 132 pounds would expend doing the following activities for 30 minutes:

activity	energy
Ironing	69 cal
Cleaning	75 cal
Walking	99 cal
Golf	129 cal
Fast walking	150 cal
Cycling	180 cal
Aerobics	195 cal
Swimming	195 cal
Running	300 cal
Sprinting	405 cal

2,000 per day thereafter to maintain her new body weight. Regular exercise will also make a huge difference; the more you can burn, the less you will need to diet.

improve your diet

For most of us, simply adopting a more balanced diet will reduce our calorie intake and lead to weight loss. Follow these simple recommendations:

Eat more starchy foods, such as bread, potatoes, rice, and pasta. Assuming these replace the fattier foods you usually eat, and you don't smother them with oil or butter, this will help reduce the amount of fat and increase the amount of fiber in your diet. For the best benefits, try to use whole-grain rice, pasta, and flour, because the energy from these foods is released more slowly in the body, making you feel fuller for longer.

Eat more fruit and vegetables, aiming for at least five servings of different fruit and vegetables a day (excluding potatoes).

As long as you don't add extra fat to your fruit and vegetables in the form of cream, butter, or oil, these changes will help reduce your fat intake and increase the amount of fiber and vitamins you consume.

cutting down on unnecessary calories

Eat fewer sugary foods, such as cookies, cakes, and chocolate bars. This will also help reduce your fat intake. If you want something sweet, aim for fresh or dried fruit instead.

make changes for life

The best way to lose weight is to try to adopt healthier eating habits that you can easily maintain all the time, not just when you are trying to lose weight. Aim to lose no more than 2 pounds per week to make sure you lose only your fat stores. People who go on crash diets lose lean muscle as well as fat and are more at risk of putting weight back on again soon afterward.

For a woman, the aim is to reduce her daily calorie intake to about 1,500 cal while she is trying to lose weight, then settle on about

Reduce the amount of fat in your diet, so you consume fewer calories. Choosing low-fat versions of dairy products, such as skim milk and low-fat yogurt, doesn't necessarily mean your food will be tasteless. Low-fat versions are available for most dairy products, including milk, cheese, yogurt, and even cream and butter.

Choose lean cuts of meat, such as Canadian bacon instead of typical fatty bacon, and chicken breasts instead of thighs. Trim all visible fat off meat before cooking and avoid frying foods—broil or roast instead. Fish is also naturally low in fat and can make a variety of tempting dishes.

simple steps to reduce your intake

Few of us have an iron will, so when you are trying to cut down, make it easier on yourself by following these steps:

- Serve small servings to start with. You may feel satisfied when you have finished, but if you are still hungry, you can go back for more.
- Once you have served your meal, put away any leftover food before you eat. Don't put serving dishes with mounds of food on the table, because you will undoubtedly pick, even if you feel satisfied with what you have already eaten.
- Eat slowly and savor your food, which should help you to feel more full when you finish eating. If you rush a meal, you may still feel hungry afterward.
- Make an effort with your meals. Just because you are cutting down doesn't mean your

meals have to be low on taste as well as calories. You will feel more satisfied with a meal you have really enjoyed and will be less tempted to look for comfort in a bag of potato chips or a bar of chocolate.

- Plan your meals in advance to make sure you have all the ingredients you need. Searching the cupboards when you are hungry is unlikely to result in a healthy, balanced meal.
- Keep healthy and interesting snacks on hand for those moments when you need something to pep you up. You don't need to succumb to a chocolate bar if there are other tempting treats available.

what is gluten and why should you avoid it?

This book aims to show you not only how you can cook foods to avoid eating gluten, but also how to eat low-calorie foods to enable you to loose or maintain your weight in a controlled and healthy way. There are plenty of gluten-free foods available to buy in supermarkets, but these are not always healthy or low in calories, so cooking ingredients from scratch is sometimes preferable, and this book shows that it can be tasty, easy, and usually cheaper, too.

Gluten is the general name for proteins found in wheat, rye, and barley, and although it has been part of the human diet for thousands of years, an increasing number of people have a negative reaction to it, especially those with celiac disease.

Celiac disease is an autoimmune disease that affects 1 in 133 people in the United States. Symptoms include chronic diarrhea, weight loss, abdominal pain, joint pain, and fatigue. Gluten triggers an immune response that causes damage to the intestines, leaving people unable to absorb nutrients from food, which in turn can lead to more serious, life-threatening problems. There is no known cure and the best treatment is to follow a gluten-free diet for life.

Millions of people who don't have celiac disease still experience negative symptoms after eating gluten—this is referred to as "gluten intolerance," and it occurs when a person's immune system responds abnormally when gluten is digested, causing uncomfortable symptoms, such as bloating, abdominal pain, and heartburn.

If you are not sure if your symptoms relate to gluten, it is best to avoid all foods that contain gluten (see below), then gradually reintroduce them to your diet to assess your body's reaction.

foods to avoid

Gluten is found in wheat, rye, and barley, as well as any foods made with these grains, such as:

- White flour
- Whole-wheat flour
- Durum wheat
- Kamut
- Spelt
- Semolina
- Wheat bran
- Wheat germ

Processed foods that contain gluten also include:
- Couscous
- Pasta
- Bread
- Flour tortillas
- Cakes
- Muffins
- Cookies
- Crackers
- Cereals
- Beer
- Gravy
- Dressings
- Sauces
- Pastries
- Baking powder
- Foods in batter

Foods that may also contain gluten but are less obvious include:
- Soy sauce
- Matzo
- Prepared soups
- Bouillon cubes
- Some confectionery

- Frankfurters
- Seasoned potato chips or snacks
- Prepared salad dressings
- Sausages

This list of foods to avoid is by no means a definitive list, because products change every day, so it is important if you are buying processed foods, to read the labels thoroughly (another good reason to cook your own foods from scratch). It is also important to remember that wheat-free does not mean gluten-free, because the food may still contain traces of rye or barley.

Cross-contamination can also occur with some foods, so again it is important to check labels carefully. For example, pure oats are gluten-free, but most commercially processed oats may be contaminated during growing, harvesting, or processing.

so what can you eat?

It may seem like there is a lot you cannot have, but it's better to focus on all the great ingredients you can eat. There are now plenty of gluten-free bread, pasta, cookie, and cake products available to buy, but you can also make your own, or substitute with something else. For example, instead of pasta, try quinoa or rice, stock up on great fresh fruit and vegetables, and use spices and herbs to add great flavors.

If you love baking and hate the thought of living without cake or cookies, there are also a number of gluten-free flours available—for example, rice, chickpea, almond, buckwheat, chestnut, tapioca, and coconut—as well as gluten-free baking powder and baking soda. The recipes in this book have been tested using gluten-free flours, but be aware that these flours act differently to normal flour, and brands of gluten-free all-purpose flour can vary, so you may need to experiment

(you may need to add up to a few tablespoons per cup given in a recipe). If adapting other recipes, it's best at first to avoid recipes that rely on flour as the main ingredient, or use ground almonds (almond meal) with gluten-free flours to help add "moisture" (see Cottage Cheese & Chive Muffins on page 126), because gluten-free flours are dry.

To begin with, eating gluten-free may seem difficult, but once you get to grips with new ingredients, you will find it can be just as simple and satisfying as eating a gluten-rich diet. Remember to seek out naturally gluten-free foods (meat, fish, seafood, eggs, dairy, and beans), and there are loads of them. Although grains that carry gluten are out, there are many naturally gluten-free grains—such as quinoa, millet, amaranth, flax, and chia—that you can enjoy in a variety of ways. For recipes using quinoa, for example, try the Quinoa & Lamb Stuffed Bell Peppers on page 100 or Turkey Balls with Minty Quinoa on page 230. Many gluten-free grains are now available at supermarkets, but some may also be found at your local health-food store.

weight loss

Gluten-free in itself is not a way to lose weight (because you can still eat sugar), so it's important to be sure your diet is still balanced—eating good protein at every meal, with fresh vegetables, salad, and fruits as accompaniments. Store-bought gluten-free foods may contain more sugar to give them extra taste and texture so, again, cooking

from scratch enables you to be in control of what you eat and makes it easier to be aware of how much sugar and calories you consume each day. Serving control is important, and in this book a calorie intake is given for each recipe for make great-tasting dishes from less than 200 to less than 500 calories per serving. If you include snacks in your daily intake, just be sure they are healthy choices.

When you are trying to lose weight, the key is to make conscious choices about eating whole, nutritious foods, with a diet that suits your lifestyle, and including exercise to balance what you eat.

less than 200 calories

caprese salad

Calories per serving **130**
Serves **4**
Preparation time **10 minutes**

4 large, ripe **beefsteak
    tomatoes**, sliced
4 **low-fat mozzarella balls**
    (about 4 oz each), sliced
handful of **basil leaves**
2 tablespoons **balsamic
    vinegar**
2 tablespoons **extra virgin
    olive oil**
black pepper

Divide the tomato slices and mozzarella slices among 4 plates, layering them alternately.

Sprinkle with the basil leaves, black pepper, vinegar, and olive oil and serve.

For tomato & basil soup, heat 1 tablespoon olive oil in a saucepan, add 1 finely chopped onion, and sauté for 2–3 minutes, then add 1 crushed garlic clove and cook for another 1 minute, until softened. Add 5 cups canned diced tomatoes, 1¼ cups chopped basil, ½ teaspoon sugar, ½ teaspoon Worcestershire sauce, and 1 tablespoon tomato paste. Mix well, then pour in 1⅔ cups boiling water and mix again. Bring to a boil, then reduce the heat and simmer for 30 minutes. Using a handhand blender, blend the soup until smooth. Ladle into 4 bowls and serve sprinkled with black pepper, a drizzle of olive oil, and a few basil leaves. **Calories per serving 131**

cauliflower & peanut salad

Calories per serving **156**
Serves **4**
Preparation time **5 minutes**
Cooking time **5 minutes**

1 **cauliflower**, broken into
  florets
1 teaspoon **mustard seeds**
small bunch of **cilantro**,
  chopped
juice of 2 **limes**
½ teaspoon **honey**
1 tablespoon **olive oil**
1 tablespoon **black sesame
  seeds**
3 tablespoons **gluten-free
  dry-roasted peanuts**,
  lightly crushed

Put the cauliflower into a steamer and steam for
3 minutes, until just tender. Place in a serving dish.

Meanwhile, heat a nonstick skillet and dry-fry the
mustard seeds until they start to pop. Set aside.

Mix together the chopped cilantro, lime juice, honey,
and olive oil in a small bowl.

Add the dressing, toasted mustard seeds, sesame
seeds, and peanuts to the cauliflower and toss together,
then serve.

For spicy cauliflower soup, heat 1 tablespoon olive
oil in a saucepan, add 1 chopped onion, and sauté
for 2–3 minutes, until softened, then add 1 teaspoon
turmeric, 1 teaspoon ground coriander, and 1 teaspoon
ground cumin. Stir in the florets of 1 cauliflower and
mix well to coat with all the spices. Pour in 6⅓ cups
hot gluten-free vegetable broth and simmer for
25–30 minutes, until tender. Using a handheld blender,
blend the soup until smooth. Ladle into 4 bowls and
serve sprinkled with 1 tablespoon chopped cilantro.
Calories per serving 143

onion, tomato & chickpea soup

Calories per serving **150**
   (not including bread)
Serves **6**
Preparation time **15 minutes**
Cooking time **1 hour**
   10 minutes

2 tablespoons **olive oil**
2 **red onions**, coarsely
   chopped
2 **garlic cloves**, finely chopped
2 teaspoons packed
   brown sugar
5 **tomatoes** (about 1¼ lb),
   skinned if preferred, coarsely
   chopped
2 teaspoons **harissa paste**
1 tablespoon **tomato paste**
1⅔ cups rinsed, drained
   canned **chickpeas**
3¾ cups **gluten-free**
   vegetable or **chicken broth**
salt and **black pepper**

Heat the oil in a large saucepan, add the onions, and sauté over low heat for 10 minutes, stirring occasionally, until just beginning to brown around the edges. Stir in the garlic and sugar and cook for another 10 minutes, stirring more frequently as the onions begin to caramelize.

Stir in the tomatoes and harissa paste and cook for 5 minutes. Mix in the tomato paste, chickpeas, broth, and salt and black pepper and bring to a boil. Cover, reduce the heat, and simmer for 45 minutes, until the tomatoes and onion are soft. Taste and adjust the seasoning, if needed.

Ladle into 6 bowls and serve with warm gluten-free tomato ciabatta, if desired.

For spicy red onion & bean soup, make the soup as above but omit the harissa and add 1 teaspoon smoked paprika and 1 split dried red chile when cooking the tomatoes. Replace the chickpeas with 1⅔ cups rinsed, drained canned red kidney beans. Serve with gluten-free garlic bread, if desired. **Calories per serving 144 (not including bread)**

24

minted spring lamb soup

Calories per serving **199**
Serves **4**
Preparation time **5 minutes**
Cooking time **10 minutes**

7⅔ cups **gluten-free vegetable broth**
5 oz **baby carrots**, peeled and sliced
2 cups shredded **cooked lamb**
1 cup **peas**
8 **scallions**, sliced
¼ cup chopped **mint**
salt and **black pepper**

Pour the broth into a saucepan and bring to a simmer. Add the carrots and cook for 3–4 minutes, then add the lamb and peas and cook for another 2 minutes, until the vegetables are tender.

Stir in the scallions and mint, then season to taste.

Ladle the soup into 4 bowls and serve.

For minted spring lamb salad, whisk together 2 tablespoons olive oil, 1 tablespoon chopped mint, 2 teaspoons lemon juice, ½ teaspoon honey, and salt and black pepper in a bowl. Put 2 cups baby spinach, ½ bunch of watercress or 2 cups of other peppery greens, and 2 sliced roasted red peppers in a salad bowl with the seeds of 1 pomegranate, ½ cup crumbled feta cheese, and 2 cups shredded cooked lamb. Toss with the dressing and serve. **Calories per serving 357**

bloody mary soup

Calories per serving **151**
Serves **6**
Preparation time **20 minutes,**
  plus chilling
Cooking time **25 minutes**

1 tablespoon **olive oil,**
  plus extra to serve
1 **onion**, chopped
1 **red bell pepper**, cored,
  seeded, and diced
2 **celery sticks**, sliced
8 **plum tomatoes** (about 1 lb),
  chopped
3¾ cups **gluten-free**
  vegetable broth
2 teaspoons **sugar**
4 teaspoons **Worcestershire**
  sauce
4 teaspoons **tomato paste**
¼ cup **vodka**
few drops of **Tabasco sauce**
salt and **black pepper**
baby celery sticks with leaves,
  to garnish

Heat the oil in a saucepan, add the onion, and sauté for 5 minutes, until softened but not browned. Stir in the red bell pepper, celery, and tomatoes and cook for 5 minutes, stirring occasionally.

Pour in the broth, add the sugar, Worcestershire sauce, tomato paste, and a little salt and black pepper, and bring to a boil. Cover and simmer for 15 minutes.

Let the soup cool slightly, then puree in batches in a blender or food processor until smooth. Strain, if desired, then pour back into the saucepan. Add the vodka and Tabasco to taste, and adjust the seasoning, if needed. Chill well.

Ladle the soup into 6 small glasses or bowls, add the baby celery sticks, drizzle with a little extra olive oil, and sprinkle with a little extra black pepper.

For Virgin Mary & pesto soup, sauté the onion in the oil as above, add the red bell pepper, celery, and tomatoes, then simmer in 3¾ cups gluten-free broth mixed with 4 teaspoons tomato paste and 2 teaspoons sugar for 15 minutes. Puree with 1 tablespoon pesto. Chill and serve with a little extra pesto added to each bowl and garnished with a few tiny basil leaves.
Calories per serving 154

smoked haddock & kale soup

Calories per serving **198**
Serves **4**
Preparation time **10 minutes**
Cooking time **20–25 minutes**

1 tablespoon **olive oil**
2 **shallots**, diced
3 **garlic cloves**, crushed
1 **large potato**, peeled
   and diced
1½ cups **unsweetened
   soy milk**
2 cups **water**
4½ cups shredded **kale**
10 oz **smoked haddock** or
   other **smoked fish**, skinned
   and chopped
salt and **black pepper**

Heat the oil in a saucepan, add the shallots and garlic, and cook for 3–4 minutes, until softened. Add the potato, milk, and measured water and season to taste. Bring to a boil, then reduce the heat and simmer for 5–6 minutes.

Stir in the kale and cook for another 10–12 minutes, until the vegetables are tender. Stir in the haddock and simmer for 2 minutes, or until cooked through.

Ladle the soup into 4 bowls and serve immediately.

For smoked haddock fish cakes with kale, cook 13 oz smoked haddock or other smoked fish under a preheated hot broiler for 4 minutes on each side, then skin and flake into a large bowl. Mix in 3 cups mashed potatoes, 1 tablespoon chopped rinsed and drained capers, the grated zest of 1 lemon, 2 tablespoons chopped parsley, and 1 beaten egg. Mix well, then shape into 8 fish cakes and dust with a little flour. Heat 2 tablespoons olive oil in a skillet and cook the fish cakes for 3–4 minutes on each side, until golden. Meanwhile, heat 2 tablespoons olive oil in a separate saucepan, add 3¾ cups chopped kale and cook for 3–4 minutes, until wilted. Serve with the fish cakes. **Calories per serving 297**

asparagus with poached eggs

Calories per serving **199**
Serves **4**
Preparation time **5 minutes**
Cooking time **6–8 minutes**

4 **eggs**
1 ½ lb **asparagus spears**
1 tablespoon **olive oil**
⅓ cup **Parmesan cheese**
  shavings

Bring a saucepan of water to a gentle simmer and stir with a large spoon to create a swirl. Break 2 eggs into the water and cook for 3–4 minutes. Remove with a slotted spoon and keep warm. Repeat with the remaining eggs.

Meanwhile, snap the woody ends off the asparagus spears and discard. Heat a ridged grill pan until hot and sprinkle it with the oil. Add the asparagus and cook, turning frequently, until slightly charred and just tender.

Divide the asparagus among 4 plates and top with the poached eggs. Sprinkle with the Parmesan shavings and serve.

For asparagus omelet, heat the oil in a skillet, add 6 trimmed and chopped asparagus spears, 2 sliced scallions, and 3–4 sliced cremini mushrooms, and cook for 5–6 minutes, until softened. Whisk together 5 eggs and ¼ cup low-fat milk in a small bowl, then pour into the pan, tilting the pan and moving the egg with a spatula to make sure it cooks evenly. Sprinkle with ¼ cup grated Parmesan, then place under a preheated hot broiler for 1–2 minutes, until golden. Cut into quarters and serve with a green salad and new potatoes, if desired. **Calories per serving 222 (not including salad and potatoes)**

veg kebabs with dipping sauce

Calories per serving **192**
Serves **4**
Preparation time **20 minutes**
Cooking time **12–15 minutes**

3 **red onions**, cut into wedges
2 **zucchini**, thickly sliced
2 **red bell peppers**, cored,
    seeded, and chopped
1 **yellow bell pepper**, cored,
    seeded, and chopped
3½ tablespoons **olive oil**
1 tablespoon **balsamic
    vinegar**
2 tablespoons chopped
    fresh herbs
salt and **black pepper**

Thread the vegetables alternately onto 8 bamboo skewers that have been presoaked in water for 10 minutes to prevent burning. Brush the vegetables with 1½ teaspoons of the oil and season well with salt and black pepper.

Cook the kebabs under a preheated hot broiler or on a barbecue grill rack for 12–15 minutes, turning frequently, until tender.

Meanwhile, make the dipping sauce. Mix together the remaining oil, vinegar, and herbs in a small bowl.

Serve the vegetable kebabs with the dipping sauce.

For quick vegetable & herb soup, heat 1 tablespoon olive oil in a saucepan over medium heat, add 1 large chopped onion, 2 sliced garlic cloves, 3 sliced celery sticks, and 2 cups finely diced butternut squash, and cook for 2–3 minutes. Pour in 1⅔ cups canned diced tomatoes and 2½ cups hot gluten-free vegetable broth and bring to a boil. Simmer for 7–8 minutes, then stir in 2 tablespoons chopped parsley. Season to taste, ladle into 4 bowls, and serve. **Calories per serving 120**

sushi triangles

Calories per serving **196**
Serves **4**
Preparation time **20 minutes**

2 cups cooked **sushi rice**
sushi rice seasoning, to taste
4 sheets of **nori seaweed**
3½ oz **smoked salmon**
½ cup thinly sliced **cucumber**

To serve
gluten-free soy sauce
wasabi

Season the rice to taste with the sushi rice seasoning.

Place 2 of the seaweed sheets onto a board. Spread one-quarter of the rice over each, cover with the smoked fish, then the cucumber. Spoon the remaining rice over the cucumber, then top with the other seaweed sheets. Press the sushi down well so the layers stick together.

Cut the sushi into 4 triangles and serve with soy sauce and wasabi.

For shrimp & roasted pepper sushi, season the rice as above, then layer onto the seaweed sheets with 3½ oz cooked peeled shrimp, 1 sliced roasted red pepper, and 1 pitted, peeled, and sliced ripe avocado. Top with the remaining seaweed sheets and continue as above. **Calories per serving 276**

salmon ceviche

Calories per serving **196**
Serves **4**
Preparation time **15 minutes,
  plus marinating**

13 oz **fresh skinless salmon
  fillet**, thinly sliced
juice of 6–8 **limes**
4 **scallions**, finely chopped
2 **celery sticks**, finely sliced
1 tablespoon finely chopped
  cilantro leaves
1 bunch of **watercress** or
  3½ cups other **peppery
  greens**, to garnish

Put the salmon into a nonmetallic bowl and cover with
the lime juice. Cover and let marinate in the refrigerator
for 25 minutes.

When ready to serve, drain the salmon, add the scallions,
celery, and cilantro, and mix well.

Garnish with the watercress and serve.

For hot-smoked salmon salad, blanch 7 oz
trimmed asparagus in a saucepan of boiling water
for 1–2 minutes, then drain and refresh under cold
running water. Whisk together 3 tablespoons extra
virgin olive oil, 1 tablespoon lime juice, 1 teaspoon
gluten-free whole-grain mustard, ½ teaspoon honey,
and 1 seeded and diced red chile in a small bowl. In
a large bowl, toss together 13 oz flaked hot-smoked
salmon, 4 sliced scallions, a small handful of cilantro
leaves, ¾ cup sliced radishes, 1 (8 oz) package mixed
salad greens, 12 halved baby plum tomatoes, the
cooked asparagus, and the salad dressing. Divide
among 4 plates and serve immediately with lime
wedges. **Calories per serving 367**

deviled chicken

Calories per serving **145**
Serves **4**
Preparation time **10 minutes**
Cooking time **16–20 minutes**

8 **boneless, skinless chicken
   thighs** (about 1 ¼ lb in total)
salad greens, to serve

Devil sauce
2 tablespoons **gluten-free
   Dijon mustard**
6 drops of **Tabasco sauce**
2 **garlic cloves**, crushed
1 tablespoon **gluten-free
   soy sauce**

Make the devil sauce. Mix together the mustard, Tabasco, garlic, and soy sauce in a shallow dish.

Open out the chicken thighs and trim away any fat. Dip the thighs in the devil sauce and coat each piece well.

Heat a large ridged grill pan or skillet. Add the chicken pieces flat on the pan and cook for 8–10 minutes on each side, until cooked through. Serve hot or cold with salad greens.

For jerk chicken, mix 3 tablespoons prepared gluten-free jerk marinade paste with the grated zest and juice of ½ orange and 2 finely chopped garlic cloves. Dip the chicken in this mixture, then cook as above. Serve with a salad. **Calories per serving 148**

spicy turkey burgers with salsa

Calories per serving **185**
Serves **4**
Preparation time **20 minutes**
Cooking time **10–12 minutes**

13 oz **ground turkey**
¾ inch piece of **fresh ginger root**, peeled and grated
4 **scallions**, finely chopped
1 **red chile**, seeded and finely chopped
1 **egg yolk**
2 tablespoons chopped **cilantro leaves**
4 **Boston, Bibb**, or other small **butterhead lettuce**

Salsa
1 **red bell pepper**, cored, seeded, and diced
1 **tomato**, diced
1 small **red onion**, finely diced
1½ teaspoons chopped **parsley**
1½ teaspoons chopped **cilantro leaves**
1 tablespoon **red wine vinegar**
1½ teaspoons **olive oil**

Mix together the ground turkey, ginger, scallions, chile, egg yolk, and cilantro in a bowl. Using wet hands, shape the mixture into 4 patties.

Heat a lightly oiled skillet and cook the patties for 5–6 minutes on each side, until golden and cooked through.

Meanwhile, for the salsa, mix together the red bell pepper, tomatoes, onion, parsley, cilantro, vinegar, and oil in a bowl.

Serve the burgers on a bed of lettuce, topped with the salsa.

For Asian turkey salad, mix together 3 finely sliced shallots with ¼ teaspoon salt and let stand for 10 minutes. Whisk together the juice of 1 lime, 2 tablespoons gluten-free Thai fish sauce, 1 tablespoon rice vinegar, 1 tablespoon sugar, 2 crushed garlic cloves, and 1 finely diced red chile. In a large bowl, toss together 2½ cups cooked turkey strips, 4¼ cups finely shredded napa cabbage, 1 large peeled and grated carrot, 1 cup bean sprouts, and a small handful each of mint and basil. Toss in the shallots and dressing and let stand for 5 minutes, then serve sprinkled with ⅓ cup chopped roasted peanuts. **Calories per serving 149**

vietnamese rice paper rolls

Calories per roll with sauce **57**
Makes **12**
Preparation time **15 minutes**

4 oz **cooked peeled shrimp**
¼ **cucumber**, cut into
   matchsticks
handful of **cilantro leaves**,
   chopped
handful of **mint**, chopped
handful of **Thai basil**, chopped
1 cup cold, cooked
   rice vermicelli
¼ **iceberg lettuce**, shredded
12 **round rice paper sheets**
lime wedges, to serve

Dipping sauce
1 tablespoon **sesame seeds**
2 tablespoons **gluten-free
   sweet chili dipping sauce**
juice of 1 **lime**
1 tablespoon **gluten-free
   Thai fish sauce**

Heat a nonstick skillet over medium-low heat and dry-fry the sesame seeds for 2 minutes, stirring frequently, until golden brown and toasted. Set aside.

Mix together the shrimp, cucumber, herbs, vermicelli, and lettuce in a large bowl.

Soak 1 rice sheet in a bowl of warm water for 20 seconds, then drain on paper towels. Fill with the shrimp mixture, leaving about 1 inch at the top and the bottom of the sheet. Fold over the top and bottom edges and roll up. Repeat with the remaining rice sheets and filling.

Whisk together the remaining dipping sauce ingredients and toasted sesame seeds in a serving dish and serve with the rolls and lime wedges.

For crab rolls, omit the shrimp and cucumber and replace with 7 oz fresh white crabmeat and 4 finely sliced scallions. Continue as above. **Calories per roll with sauce 67**

44

smoked salmon sesame blinis

Calories per blini **50**
Makes **25**
Preparation time **10 minutes,**
   plus chilling
Cooking time **10 minutes**

⅔ cup **gluten-free**
   all-purpose flour
1 **egg**
⅔ cup **soy yogurt**
2 tablespoons **cold water**
1 **red chile**, seeded and
   chopped
8 **scallions**, finely sliced
2 tablespoons chopped
   cilantro leaves
1 tablespoon **sesame seeds**
1 tablespoon **sunflower oil**
¼ cup **reduced-fat crème**
   fraîche or **sour cream**
5 oz **smoked salmon**, sliced
salt and **black pepper**
chopped **chives**, to garnish

Put the flour, egg, yogurt, and measured water into a blender or food processor and process to form a smooth batter. Pour into a bowl, then stir in the chile, scallions, cilantro, sesame seeds, and salt and black pepper. Cover and chill for 20 minutes.

Heat a skillet with a little of the oil and then wipe with paper towels. Add tablespoonfuls of the batter and cook for 1 minute on each side, until lightly golden, then remove from the pan and keep warm. Repeat with the remaining batter.

Top each blini with a little dollop of crème fraîche, a piece of smoked salmon, and a sprinkling of chopped chives and sprinkle with a little extra black pepper.

For broiled sesame salmon, whisk together 2 tablespoons gluten-free soy sauce, 2 teaspoons honey, 2 teaspoons peeled and grated fresh ginger root, 1 tablespoon sesame oil, and 2 crushed garlic cloves. Put 4 salmon fillets (about 5 oz each) into a shallow bowl and pour the marinade over them. Cover and let marinate in the refrigerator for 10–15 minutes. Cook the salmon fillets, skin side up, under a preheated broiler for 5–6 minutes, then turn the fillets over, sprinkle with 2 tablespoons sesame seeds, and cook for another 3–4 minutes, until golden and cooked through. Serve with a crisp green salad. **Calories per serving 351**

carrot & cumin crispbreads

Calories per crispbread **99**

Makes **20**

Preparation time **15 minutes**

Cooking time **30 minutes**

⅓ cup **sunflower seeds**

⅓ cup **pumpkin seeds**

⅓ cup **sesame seeds**

⅔ cup **whole almonds**, toasted

1½ tablespoons **cumin seeds**

2 **carrots**, peeled and shredded

3 tablespoons **pesto**

1 tablespoon **olive oil**, plus extra for greasing

2–3 tablespoons **cold water**

Put the sunflower, pumpkin and sesame seeds, almonds, and 1 tablespoon of the cumin seeds into a blender or food processor and pulse until broken down. Add the grated carrots, pesto, oil, and measured water and process until a thick paste forms.

Spread the crispbread mixture over a greased baking sheet to about ¼ inch thick, then score into 20 rectangles and sprinkle with the remaining cumin seeds. Bake in a preheated oven, at 400°F, for 25 minutes, until golden and firm.

Cut through the score lines to separate the crispbreads, then turn over and bake for another 5–6 minutes, until crisp and golden. Transfer to a wire rack and let cool. Store in an airtight container and eat within 4–5 days.

For carrot & cumin soup, dry-fry 2 teaspoons cumin seeds in a saucepan, then add 1 tablespoon olive oil, 4⅓ cups peeled and chopped carrots (about 1¼ lb), ⅔ cup red lentils, and 4¼ cups gluten-free vegetable broth and bring to a boil. Reduce the heat and simmer for 15–18 minutes, until the carrots are tender and the lentils are swollen and soft. Using a handheld blender, blend the soup until smooth. Ladle into 4 bowls and serve sprinkled with 2 tablespoons toasted pumpkin seeds and 1 tablespoon chopped parsley. **Calories per serving 251**

spicy corn bread

Calories per square **115**
Makes **16** squares
Preparation time **5 minutes**
Cooking time **30–35 minutes**

3 tablespoons **olive oil**,
   plus extra for greasing
1 cup **rice flour**
1 cup plus 1 tablespoon
   cornmeal
1 teaspoon **salt**
2 teaspoons **gluten-free**
   baking powder
1 tablespoon **sugar**
3 tablespoons grated
   Parmesan cheese
handful of **fresh herbs**,
   chopped
1 **red chile**, seeded and
   finely chopped
2 **eggs**, beaten
1¼ cups **buttermilk**

Grease an 8 inch square cake pan with olive oil.

Sift together the flour, cornmeal, salt, and baking powder into a large bowl. Stir in the sugar, Parmesan, herbs, and chile.

Mix together the oil, eggs, and buttermilk in a separate bowl, then pour into the dry ingredients and gently stir until combined.

Pour the batter into the prepared pan and bake in a preheated oven, at 375°F, for 30–35 minutes, until golden. Transfer to a wire rack and let cool, then cut into 16 squares. The bread is best eaten on the same day.

For bacon & corn bread, stir in 1¼ cups drained canned corn kernels and 6 chopped broiled bacon strips into the dry ingredients and continue as above. Calories per square 150

carrot & lentil muffins

Calories per muffin **141**
Makes **12**
Preparation time **15 minutes**
Cooking time **25–30 minutes**

⅓ cup **red lentils**
1 cup plus 3 tablespoons
  water
1¾ cups **gluten-free**
  all-purpose flour
2 tablespoons **ground**
  flaxseed
1½ teaspoons **gluten-free**
  baking powder
¼ cup packed **dark**
  brown sugar
1 teaspoon **ground cinnamon**
½ teaspoon **ground cloves**
3 tablespoons **prepared**
  gluten-free applesauce
3 tablespoons **honey**
3 tablespoons **sunflower oil**
1 **egg**
1 large **carrot**, peeled and
  shredded
2–3 tablespoons **soy milk**
  (optional)

Line a 12-cup muffin pan with paper muffin liners.

Put the lentils and measured water into a saucepan, bring to a boil, then reduce the heat and simmer for 8 minutes, until soft. Drain.

Sift the flour, flaxseed, and baking powder into a large bowl, then stir in the sugar and spices.

Put the drained lentils into a blender or food processor with the applesauce, honey, oil, and egg and blend until smooth.

Pour the wet ingredients into the dry, stirring in the shredded carrots when nearly blended. Add the soy milk to loosen the batter, if needed.

Spoon the batter into the muffin liners and bake in a preheated oven, at 350°F, for 18–20 minutes, until risen and golden. Transfer to a wire rack and let cool.

For carrot & lentil soup, dry-fry 2 teaspoons cumin seeds and a pinch of dried red pepper flakes in a small skillet for 1 minute. Heat 1 tablespoon olive oil in a saucepan, then add half of the spices, 5½ cups peeled and shredded carrots (about 1¼ lb), 1¾ cups red lentils, 4¼ cups gluten-free vegetable broth, and ½ cup milk to the pan and bring to a boil. Simmer for 12–15 minutes, until the lentils are soft and swollen. Using a handheld blender, blend the soup until smooth. Ladle into 4 bowls, drizzle each with 2 tablespoons plain yogurt, then serve with a few cilantro leaves and the remaining spices sprinkled over the top. **Calories per serving 250**

lemon cookies

Calories per cookie **146**
Makes **20**
Preparation time **20 minutes**
Cooking time **12–15 minutes**

½ cup **oil**
¼ cup **soy yogurt**
3 **lemons**
½ cup firmly packed **light brown sugar**
1 cup plus 1 tablespoon **gluten-free all-purpose flour**
1 cup **gluten-free rolled oats**
⅓ cup plus 1 tablespoon **millet flakes**
½ cup **unsweetened dried coconut**, plus 1 tablespoon for dusting

Mix together the olive oil, yogurt, juice of 1 lemon, and grated zest of 2 lemons in a bowl. In a separate bowl, mix together the sugar, flour, oats, millet, and coconut.

Stir the wet ingredients into the dry ingredients and mix to form a soft dough.

Roll the dough into 20 balls, then place on a baking sheet and press down gently. Sprinkle the cookies with the remaining dried coconut and the grated zest of 1 lemon.

Bake the cookies in a preheated oven, at 350°F, for 12–15 minutes, until golden. Let cool on the sheet for a few minutes, then transfer to a wire rack and let cool completely. Store in an airtight container and eat within 2–3 days.

For lemon posset, mix together 1⅔ cups fat-free Greek yogurt, 1 tablespoon confectioners' sugar, the grated zest of 3 lemons, and 2 teaspoons lemon juice in a bowl. Spoon into 4 small glasses or bowls and chill for at least 1 hour. Sprinkle 1 tablespoon unsweetened dried coconut over the possets, then serve each with 1 lemon cookie (see above). **Calories per serving 238**

orange shortbread cookies

Calories per cookie **59**

Makes **10**

Preparation time **10 minutes, plus chilling**

Cooking time **12–15 minutes**

7 tablespoons **unsalted butter**, softened, plus extra for greasing

¼ cup **sugar**

grated zest of 1 **orange**

1 cup plus 2 tablespoons **gluten-free all-purpose flour**

½ teaspoon **gluten-free baking powder**

Beat the butter in a bowl until soft, then cream together with the sugar and orange zest until light and fluffy. Stir in the flour and baking powder and mix to form a light dough.

Roll the dough into a circle about ¼ inch thick and decorate the edge with the back of a fork. Cut into 10 wedges and place on a greased baking sheet. Chill for 15 minutes.

Bake the cookies in a preheated oven, at 375°F, for 12–15 minutes, until golden. Let cool on the baking sheet for 2 minutes, then transfer to a wire rack and let cool completely. Store in an airtight container and eat within 3–4 days.

For amaretti orange dessert, divide 10 crumbled gluten-free amaretti cookies among 4 glasses or small bowls. Stir the grated zest of 4 oranges into 1⅔ cups fat-free Greek yogurt. Divide the 4 grated oranges into sections over a bowl to catch the juice, then put the orange sections on top of the crushed cookies and pour any juice over them. Top with the yogurt and sprinkle each one with 1 teaspoon brown sugar. Chill for 20 minutes before serving. **Calories per serving 204**

balsamic strawberries & mango

Calories per serving **109**
Serves **4**
Preparation time **5 minutes,
plus overnight chilling and
standing**

3¼ cups **strawberries**
(about 1 lb)
1 large **mango**, peeled, pitted,
and sliced
1−2 tablespoons **sugar**
3 tablespoons **balsamic
vinegar**
2 tablespoons chopped **mint**,
to decorate

Mix together the strawberries and mango in a large,
shallow nonmetallic bowl, sprinkle with the sugar,
according to taste, and pour the vinegar over the fruit.
Cover with plastic wrap and chill overnight.

Remove the fruit from the refrigerator and let stand
for at least 1 hour before serving.

Spoon the fruit into 4 serving bowls, drizzle with the
syrup, and serve sprinkled with the mint.

For peppery strawberries & blueberries, mix the
strawberries with 1 cup blueberries and make as above.
Sprinkle with a few grinds of black pepper and the
chopped mint before serving. **Calories per serving 83**

chocolate orange mousse

Calories per serving **189**
Serves **4**
Preparation time **15 minutes,**
  plus cooling and chilling
Cooking time **5 minutes**

3 oz **gluten-free semisweet**
  chocolate, chopped
1 tablespoon **gluten-free**
  unsweetened cocoa
  powder
½ teaspoon **gluten-free**
  coffee granules
grated zest of **1 orange**
2 tablespoons **water**
2 **egg whites**
1 tablespoon **sugar**
¼ cup **fat-free Greek yogurt**
raspberries, to serve

Melt the chocolate in a bowl set over a saucepan of gently simmering water, making sure the bottom of the bowl does not touch the water. Stir occasionally, then let cool.

Mix together the cocoa powder, coffee, orange zest, and measured water in a small bowl, then add to the melted chocolate.

Whisk the egg whites in a clean bowl until they form soft peaks, then add the sugar and continue to whisk until thick and glossy.

Stir the yogurt into the cooled chocolate mixture, then fold in one-quarter of the egg whites. Gently fold in the remaining whites until evenly mixed.

Spoon into 4 ramekins or glasses and chill for 2 hours before serving, topped with raspberries.

For homemade chocolate orange, grate the zest from 1 orange and reserve. Cut the orange in half, scoop out the flesh, and discard, then line the halves with plastic wrap. Melt 7 oz gluten-free semisweet chocolate, 1½ tablespoons unsalted butter, and the reserved orange zest in a heatproof bowl set over a saucepan of gently simmering water. Pour the chocolate mixture into the orange halves and let set in a cool place for a few hours. Using the plastic wrap, lift out the chocolate halves, peel off the plastic wrap, and cut into 10 wedges to serve. **Calories per wedge 129**

elderflower poached pears

Calories per serving **191**
Serves **4**
Preparation time **5 minutes,
    plus cooling**
Cooking time **25 minutes**

½ cup **elderflower and apple
    cordial** or **syrup** (available
    online)
2 cups **apple juice**
2 teaspoons **lemon juice**
4 large **pears**, peeled, cored,
    and quartered
pinch of **saffron** threads

Mix the cordial or syrup, apple juice, and lemon juice in
a small, deep saucepan. Bring to a gentle simmer and
add the pears and saffron. Simmer gently for about
25 minutes or until the pears are tender.

Remove from the heat, cover, and let cool completely
in the poaching liquid. Carefully remove the pears with
a slotted spoon and divide among 4 serving bowls.
Ladle the poaching liquid over the fruit to serve.

For baked apples in elderflower & saffron, replace
the pears with 4 peeled, cored, and quartered apples
and put into a deep ovenproof dish. Heat the cordial or
syrup, apple juice, and saffron as above, omitting the
lemon juice, and pour the syrup over the apples. Cover
with aluminum foil and put into a preheated oven, at
350 °C, for about 1 hour or until the apples are tender.
Calories per serving 175

mango & passion fruit roll

Calories per serving **199**
Serves **6**
Preparation time **20 minutes,
plus standing**
Cooking time **30 minutes**

3 **extra-large egg whites**
¾ cup plus 2 tablespoons
superfine sugar
1 teaspoon **cornstarch**
1 teaspoon **white wine
vinegar**
3 tablespoon **confectioners'
sugar**
1 cup **fat-free Greek yogurt**
1 large ripe **mango**, peeled,
pitted and diced
4 **passion fruits**, pulp only

Line a 9 inch x 13 inch jellyroll pan with nonstick parchment paper.

Whisk the egg whites in a large clean bowl until frothy and doubled in size. Add the sugar, a spoonful at a time, and continue to whisk until thick and glossy. Mix together the cornstarch and vinegar in a small bowl, then whisk into the meringue mixture. Spoon into the prepared pan and gently level the surface.

Bake in a preheated oven, at 300°F, for 30 minutes, until the meringue is just firm. Remove from the oven and cover with a sheet of damp wax paper for 6–8 minutes.

Dust another sheet of wax paper with confectioners' sugar and turn the meringue out onto it, discarding the damp sheet. Peel off the lining paper.

Spread the yogurt over the meringue, then sprinkle with the mango and passion fruit pulp.

Using the paper to help, roll up the meringue from one short end. Transfer to a serving plate, seam side down, and sift a little confectioners' sugar over to serve.

For mango & passion fruit brûlée, divide 1 large peeled, pitted, and diced ripe mango and the pulp of 4 passion fruits among 6 ramekins. Top each one with 2 tablespoons fat-free Greek yogurt and sprinkle with 1½ teaspoons packed dark brown sugar. Chill for 15 minutes before serving. **Calories per serving 113**

instant mixed berry sorbet

Calories per serving **178**
Serves **4**
Preparation time **10 minutes**

2⅔ cups **frozen mixed berries**
1⅔ cups **raspberry yogurt**
⅓ cup **confectioners' sugar**

Put the frozen berries, yogurt, and confectioners' sugar into a food processor or blender. Process until blended. Scrape the mixture from the sides and blend again.

Spoon the sorbet into 4 chilled glasses or bowls and serve immediately.

For frozen berries with white & dark hot chocolate sauce, divide 3½ cups frozen mixed berries among 4 chilled serving plates or shallow bowls. Melt 3 oz gluten-free semisweet chocolate and 3 oz gluten-free white chocolate in 2 separate small saucepans. Whip ⅔ cup heavy cream until soft peaks form. When ready to serve, drizzle the hot chocolate sauces over the frozen berries and serve immediately with a dollop of the whipped cream. **Calories per serving 496**

less than
300 calories

pear & blue cheese salad

Calories per serving **295**
Serves **4**
Preparation time **15 minutes**

1 bunch **watercress** or
   3½ cups other **peppery
   greens**
2 **heads of endive**, sliced
3 **pears**, cored and sliced
¼ **cucumber**, sliced
juice of 1 **lemon**
½ teaspoon **honey**
½ teaspoon **gluten-free
   whole-grain mustard**
2 tablespoons **extra virgin
   olive oil**
⅔ cup crumbled **Stilton** or
   other **blue cheese**
2 tablespoons **chopped
   walnuts**

Toss together the watercress, endive, pears, and
cucumber and place on a serving plate or in a large
salad bowl.

Whisk together the lemon juice, honey, mustard,
and olive oil in a small bowl, then drizzle the dressing
over the salad. Sprinkle with the cheese and walnuts
and serve.

For blue cheese & pear soup, melt 1 tablespoon
butter in a saucepan, add 1 chopped onion, and sauté
for 2–3 minutes, until softened. Add 4 peeled, cored,
and chopped pears and 3½ cups gluten-free vegetable
broth and bring to a boil, then reduce the heat and
simmer for 15–18 minutes, until the pears are tender.
Using a handheld blender, blend the soup until smooth.
Return to the heat, add ¾ cup crumbled Stilton or
other blue cheese, and stir until it melts. Add a squeeze
of lemon juice and season to taste. Serve sprinkled
with 1 tablespoon chopped chives. **Calories per
serving 268**

beef carpaccio & bean salad

Calories per serving **275**
Serves **4**
Preparation time **15 minutes,
  plus freezing**
Cooking time **2–3 minutes**

8 oz **tenderloin steak**
3 tablespoons **extra virgin
  olive oil**
1 teaspoon **black pepper**
1 tablespoon chopped **thyme
  leaves**
1 teaspoon **gluten-free
  Dijon mustard**
1½ teaspoons **balsamic
  vinegar**
½ teaspoon **honey**
1 cup trimmed **green beans**
1⅔ cups rinsed, drained
  canned **cannellini (white
  kidney) beans**
1 small **red onion**, thinly sliced
¼ cup **Parmesan cheese**
  shavings, to garnish

Place the steak on a cutting board and rub with
1 tablespoon of the oil, the black pepper, and thyme.
Wrap in plastic wrap and put into the freezer for
20 minutes.

Meanwhile, whisk together the remaining oil with
the mustard, vinegar, and honey in a bowl.

Blanch the green beans for 2–3 minutes in boiling
water, then refresh under cold running water. Toss
the green beans, cannellini beans, and sliced onion
in the dressing and let stand at room temperature.

Divide the bean salad, with all the dressing, among
4 plates. Unwrap the steak, slice as thinly as possible,
and arrange the slices over the salad, then garnish with
shavings of Parmesan.

For nutty beef & bean salad, rub 14½ oz sirloin steak
with 1 tablespoon olive oil and sprinkle with 1 tablespoon
black pepper. Cook the steak for 1–2 minutes on each
side in 1 tablespoon olive oil, then let rest. In a large
bowl, toss together 1½ cups mâche or other mild
greens, 2 chopped, cooked fresh beets, 4 sliced scallions,
1⅔ cups rinsed, drained canned lima beans, 12 halved
baby plum tomatoes, and 2 tablespoons toasted
cashew nuts. Whisk together 3 tablespoons extra virgin
olive oil, 1 tablespoon balsamic vinegar, 1 crushed
garlic clove,1 teaspoon packed dark brown sugar, and
½ teaspoon gluten-free whole-grain mustard in a bowl,
then stir in 1 tablespoon coarsely chopped peanuts.
Slice the steak and place on top of the salad, then pour
the dressing over it to serve. **Calories per serving 460**

peach, feta & watercress salad

Calories per serving **259**
Serves **4**
Preparation time **10 minutes**
Cooking time **2–3 minutes**

3 tablespoons **pumpkin
    seeds**
juice of ½ **lemon**
2 tablespoons **extra virgin
    olive oil**
½ teaspoon **gluten-free
    Dijon mustard**
1 teaspoon **honey**
1 tablespoon chopped
    oregano
¾ bunch of **watercress** or
    3 cups other **peppery
    greens**
3 **peaches**, halved, pitted,
    and sliced
4 **scallions**, sliced
1 cup plus 2 tablespoons
    crumbled **feta cheese**
black pepper

Heat a nonstick skillet over medium-low heat and dry-fry the pumpkin seeds for 2–3 minutes, stirring frequently, until slightly golden and toasted. Set aside.

Whisk together the lemon juice, oil, mustard, honey, oregano, and black pepper in a small bowl.

Divide the watercress among 4 plates, top with the peach slices and scallions, then sprinkle with the feta cheese.

Serve sprinkled with the toasted pumpkin seeds and drizzled with the dressing.

For peach, feta & watercress bruschetta, cut
2 gluten-free baguettes into ¾ inch slices. Put the slices onto a baking sheet and drizzle with 2 tablespoons olive oil. Bake in a preheated oven, at 400°F, for 10–12 minutes, until golden. Rub one side of each slice with a garlic clove. Halve, pit, and slice 4 peaches. Top the toasts with a few watercress sprigs, the peach slices, and ¾ cup crumbled feta cheese. Serve drizzled with balsamic glaze. **Calories per serving 384**

monkfish kebabs with tabbouleh

Calories per serving **285**
Serves **4**
Preparation time **20 minutes,
plus marinating**
Cooking time **25–30 minutes**

1½ inch piece of **fresh ginger
root**, peeled and diced
grated zest and juice of
1 **lemon**
½ teaspoon **turmeric**
2 **garlic cloves**, crushed
½ teaspoon **dried red
pepper flakes**
1 tablespoon chopped **mint**
¼ cup **plain yogurt**
1 lb **monkfish**, skinned and
cut into bite-size chunks
1¼ cups **quinoa**
¼ cup chopped **parsley**
2 tablespoons chopped
cilantro leaves
3 **cherry tomatoes**, quartered
lemon wedges, to serve

Mix together the ginger, lemon zest and juice, turmeric, garlic, red pepper flakes, half the mint, and the yogurt in a small bowl.

Thread the monkfish onto 8 bamboo skewers that have been presoaked in water for 10 minutes to prevent burning, then place in a shallow nonmetallic dish. Pour the yogurt marinade over the skewers and let marinate for 20 minutes.

Meanwhile, cook the quinoa in a saucepan of boiling water according to the package directions, then drain and refresh under cold running water and drain again. Transfer to a bowl and stir in the remaining mint, the parsley, cilantro, and tomatoes.

Cook the kebabs under a preheated hot broiler or on a barbecue grill rack for 10–12 minutes, turning frequently, until the fish is cooked through. Serve with the tabbouleh and lemon wedges.

For monkfish & mango salad, toss together 13 oz monkfish, cut into chunks, 2 tablespoons olive oil, and 1 tablespoon red Thai curry paste in a bowl and let marinate for 20 minutes. Meanwhile, toss together the leaves of 2 Boston, Bibb, or other small butterhead lettuce, 1 peeled, pitted, and sliced mango, ¼ sliced cucumber, a small bunch of chopped cilantro, and 3 sliced scallions and transfer to a large serving plate. Heat a skillet (or barbecue grill) and cook the monkfish for 2–3 minutes on each side, until cooked through. Spoon onto the salad and serve sprinkled with 1 tablespoon toasted almond flakes, a squeeze of lime juice, and a drizzle of olive oil. **Calories per serving 234**

butternut & cumin soup

Calories per serving **221**
Serves **4**
Preparation time **10 minutes**
Cooking time **40–45 minutes**

2 tablespoons **pumpkin
seeds**
1 **butternut squash** (about
2 lb), peeled, seeded,
and chopped
1½ tablespoons **olive oil**
1 teaspoon **dried red
pepper flakes**
2 teaspoons **cumin seeds**
1 **onion**, chopped
1 **garlic clove**, chopped
2½ cups hot **gluten-free
vegetable broth**
2 tablespoons **plain yogurt**

Heat a nonstick skillet over medium-low heat and
dry-fry the pumpkin seeds for 2–3 minutes, stirring
frequently, until slightly golden and toasted. Set aside.

Put the squash into a roasting pan, drizzle with
1 tablespoon of the oil, and sprinkle with the red
pepper flakes and cumin seeds. Roast in a preheated
oven, at 400°F, for 30–35 minutes until tender,
tossing occasionally.

Heat the remaining oil in a saucepan, add the onion
and garlic, and sauté for 3–4 minutes. Add the squash
and broth and simmer for 5 minutes. Using a handheld
blender, blend the soup until smooth, adding more
liquid to loosen, if necessary.

Ladle the soup into 4 bowls and serve topped with
dollops of the yogurt and the toasted pumpkin seeds.

For roasted butternut & cumin salad, put the
butternut squash, cut into wedges, into a roasting pan
and add the oil and cumin seeds, omitting the red
pepper flakes. Roast as above. Toss the roasted squash
with ¾ bunch of watercress or 3 cups of other peppery
greens, 12 halved cherry tomatoes, ¾ cup sugar snap
peas, and 1 cored, seeded, and sliced red bell pepper in
a serving bowl. Drizzle with 2 tablespoons gluten-free
low-fat dressing and serve. **Calories per serving 172**

caribbean pepper pot soup

Calories per serving **279**
Serves **6**
Preparation time **20 minutes**
Cooking time **45–50 minutes**

2 tablespoons **olive oil**
1 **onion**, finely chopped
1 **Scotch bonnet chile**,
    seeded and finely chopped,
    or 2 **hot Thai red chiles**,
    chopped with seeds
2 **red bell peppers**, cored,
    seeded, and diced
2 **garlic cloves**, finely chopped
1 large **carrot**, peeled and
    diced
2 **Yukon Gold** or **white round
    potatoes**, peeled and diced
1 **bay leaf**
1 **thyme sprig**
1⅔ cups **coconut milk**
2½ cups **gluten-free beef
    broth**
salt and **cayenne pepper**

To serve
7 oz **sirloin steak**
2 teaspoons **olive oil**

Heat the oil in a saucepan, add the onion, and sauté gently for 5 minutes, until softened and just beginning to turn golden. Stir in the chile, red bell peppers, garlic, carrot, potatoes, and herbs and cook for 5 minutes, stirring.

Pour in the coconut milk and broth, then season with salt and cayenne pepper. Bring to a boil, stirring, then reduce the heat, cover, and simmer for 30 minutes, or until the vegetables are tender. Discard the herbs, then taste and adjust the seasoning, if needed.

Rub the steak with the oil, then season lightly with salt and cayenne pepper. Heat a ridged grill pan or skillet until hot, then add the steak and cook for 2–5 minutes on each side, until cooked to your preference. Let stand for 5 minutes, then slice thinly.

Ladle the soup into 6 bowls and top with the steak slices.

For shrimp & spinach pepper pot soup, make the soup as above using 2½ cups gluten-free fish broth in place of the beef broth. Simmer for 30 minutes, then add 7 oz raw peeled shrimp, defrosted if frozen, and 4 cups spinach. Cook for 3–4 minutes, until the shrimp turn pink and are cooked through and the spinach is just wilted. **Calories per serving 271**

shrimp with spicy dip

Calories per serving **227**
Serves **4**
Preparation time **10 minutes**

2 **Boston, Bibb,** or other small
  butterhead lettuce, leaves
  separated
13 oz **cooked peeled
  jumbo shrimp**

Spicy dip

¾ cup plus 1 tablespoon
  cream cheese
⅓ cup plus 1 tablespoon
  plain yogurt
1 **garlic clove,** crushed
2–3 drops of **lemon juice**
¼ teaspoon **dried red
  pepper flakes**
handful of snipped **chives**
salt and **black pepper**

Make the spicy dip. Mix together the cream cheese, yogurt, garlic, lemon juice, red pepper flakes, and chives in a serving bowl. Season with salt and black pepper to taste.

Arrange the lettuce on 4 small plates and top with the shrimp. Serve the dip for everyone to share.

For spicy shrimp salad, heat 2 tablespoons olive oil in a saucepan, add 1 tablespoon dried red pepper flakes and 2 crushed garlic cloves, and cook for 2 minutes. Add 1 lb raw peeled jumbo shrimp and cook for another 5–6 minutes, until the shrimp turn pink and are cooked through. Add a splash of white wine and cook until it has evaporated. Remove from the heat. Toss 3 cups arugula leaves in 2 tablespoons olive oil and 1 tablespoon balsamic vinegar. Divide among 4 plates and top with 2 peeled, pitted, and sliced avocados. Spoon the shrimp over the salad and serve sprinkled with 1 tablespoon toasted sesame seeds.
Calories per serving 385

onion bhajis

Calories per serving **213**
  (not including mango
  chutney)
Serves **4**
Preparation time **10 minutes**
Cooking time **10 minutes**

⅔ cup **chickpea flour**
3 tablespoons **rice flour**
1 tablespoon **butter**, melted
juice of ½ **lemon**
1 teaspoon **cumin seeds**
½ teaspoon **fennel seeds**
½ teaspoon **dried red**
  pepper flakes
½ teaspoon **turmeric**
2 **garlic cloves**, chopped
small bunch of **cilantro**,
  chopped
¾ inch piece of **fresh ginger**
  root, peeled and grated
2 **onions**, thinly sliced
4¼ cups **sunflower** or
  vegetable oil
salt and **black pepper**

Sift the flours into a bowl, then stir in the butter and lemon juice. Add enough cold water to make a batter the consistency of heavy cream. Stir in all the remaining ingredients except the oil, season, and mix well.

Heat the oil in a deep saucepan to 350–375°F, or until a drop of batter sizzles in the hot oil. Using 2 tablespoons, gently spoon one-eighth of the batter into the oil, then repeat until there are 3 or 4 dollops; try not to overcrowd the pan. Cook for 4–5 minutes, turning occasionally, until crisp and golden. Drain on paper towels and keep warm. Repeat with the remaining batter to make 8 bhajis.

Serve with gluten-free mango chutney, if desired.

For onion soup, heat 1 tablespoon olive oil in a skillet, add 2 crushed garlic cloves, and cook for 1 minute. Add 2 diced onions and ½ teaspoon paprika and cook for 5 minutes, until softened, then stir in 3¾ cups gluten-free chicken broth and bring to a boil. Reduce the heat and simmer for about 30 minutes. Meanwhile, poach 4 eggs (see page 32). Season the soup to taste and ladle into 4 bowls. Top each with a poached egg and cilantro sprig. **Calories per serving 165**

roasted bell peppers

Calories per serving **211**
Serves **4**
Preparation time **10 minutes**
Cooking time **25 minutes**

2 **red bell peppers**, halved,
   cored, and seeded
2 **yellow bell peppers**, halved,
   cored, and seeded
1 small **red onion**, cut into
   8 wedges
2 **runner beans**, trimmed and
   cut into small batons
1 **zucchini**, halved and sliced
3 **garlic cloves**, sliced
2 tablespoons **extra virgin
   olive oil**
1 teaspoon **cumin seeds**
4 oz **feta** or **goat cheese**
salt and **black pepper**

Place the bell pepper halves in a roasting pan and divide the other vegetables and garlic among them.

Sprinkle with the oil and cumin seeds, season with salt and black pepper, and bake in a preheated oven, at 400°F, for 25 minutes, until tender. Crumble the cheese over the top and serve.

For red bell pepper hummus, put 1⅔ cups rinsed, drained canned chickpeas into a blender or food processor and add the juice of ½ lemon, 2 crushed garlic cloves, 1 teaspoon ground cumin, 2 drained roasted red peppers from a jar, 2 tablespoons tahini paste, and 2–3 tablespoons olive oil. Blend until smooth, adding a little more olive oil if you want to loosen the texture. Serve the hummus with vegetable sticks. **Calories per serving 310**

guacamole

Calories per serving **207**
**(not including oat cakes or
vegetable sticks)**
Serves **4**
Preparation time **10 minutes**

2 **avocados**, peeled, pitted,
and chopped
juice of **1 lime**
6 **cherry tomatoes**, diced
1 tablespoon chopped
cilantro leaves
1–2 **garlic cloves**, crushed
gluten-free oat cakes, **rice
cakes**, or **vegetable sticks**,
such as **cucumber**, **bell
peppers**, and **carrots**,
to serve

Put the avocados and lime juice into a bowl and mash
together to prevent discoloration, then stir in the
remaining ingredients.

Serve immediately with gluten-free oat or rice cakes,
or with vegetable sticks, if desired.

For shrimp & avocado salad, soak 7 oz vermicelli
rice noodles in boiling water until just tender. Drain,
refresh under cold running water, and drain again, then
put into a bowl with 7 oz cooked, peeled jumbo shrimp,
2 peeled, pitted, and sliced avocados, ½ thinly sliced
cucumber, and 4 sliced scallions. Whisk together ½ cup
coconut milk, the juice of 1 lime, and a ¾ inch piece
of fresh ginger root, peeled and grated, in a separate
bowl. Pour the dressing over the salad and gently toss
together to serve. **Calories per serving 445**

trout & dill fish cakes

Calories per serving **286**
Serves **4**
Preparation time **15 minutes,
    plus chilling**
Cooking time **25–30 minutes**

10 oz **trout fillets**
2 cups **mashed potatoes**
5 **scallions**, finely chopped
2 tablespoons **capers**,
    chopped
3 tablespoons chopped **dill**
grated zest and juice of
    1 **lemon**
1 tablespoon **olive oil**
salt and **black pepper**

To serve
steamed **baby broccoli**
lime wedges

Cook the trout fillets under a preheated hot broiler
for 4 minutes on each side, until cooked through, then
discard the skin, break the flesh into flakes, and put
into a bowl.

Add the mashed potatoes, scallions, capers, dill, lemon
zest, and 2 tablespoons of lemon juice. Season with
salt and black pepper. Shape into 8 cakes and chill
for 20 minutes.

Heat the oil in a skillet and cook the fish cakes, in
batches, for 4–5 minutes on each side or until golden
and cooked through. Serve with steamed baby broccoli
and lime wedges.

For trout & dill pâté, mix together 10 oz cooked
and flaked trout fillets, 1 teaspoon gluten-free Dijon
mustard, 1 tablespoon chopped dill, 1 ¼ cups low-fat
cream cheese, and a pinch of paprika in a bowl. Season
to taste. Spoon into 4 ramekins and chill for 30 minutes.
Serve with vegetable sticks. **Calories per serving 230**

smoked salmon scrambled eggs

Calories per serving **233**
  (not including toast)
Serves **4**
Preparation time **5 minutes**
Cooking time **5 minutes**

8 **eggs**
2 tablespoons **fromage frais**
  or **low-fat plain Greek**
  yogurt
1 tablespoon chopped **chives**
4 oz **smoked salmon**, cut
  into strips
salt and **black pepper**

Whisk together the eggs, fromage frais, and salt and black pepper in a bowl.

Heat a saucepan over medium heat, pour in the egg mixture, and cook for 1 minute, then using a spatula, gently push the egg around to be sure it cooks evenly.

When the egg looks like creamy curds, stir in the chives and smoked salmon and serve immediately on buttered gluten-free toast, if desired.

For smoked salmon frittata, thickly slice 1 lb new potatoes and cook in a saucepan of boiling water for 8–10 minutes. Drain. Lightly beat 8 extra-large eggs, then stir in 7 oz strips of smoked salmon, 2 tablespoons chopped dill, ⅔ cup baby peas, and the potatoes. Season. Heat 2 tablespoons olive oil in a skillet with an ovenproof handle. Pour in the egg mixture and cook for 10–15 minutes over low heat until the egg is starting to set. Place under a preheated medium broiler and cook for 3–4 minutes, or until the egg is set and the top is golden. Turn out onto a board and cut into wedges to serve. **Calories per serving 393**

spanish-style seafood

Calories per serving **214**
 (not including bread)
Serves **4**
Preparation time **15 minutes**
Cooking time **35–40 minutes**

1 tablespoon **olive oil**
2 **garlic cloves**, sliced
1 **fennel bulb**, sliced
3½ cups **cherry tomatoes**
 (about 1 lb)
3 tablespoons **sherry**
1 tablespoon **tomato paste**
16 large **fresh mussels**,
 scrubbed and debearded
 (discard any that don't shut
 when tapped)
16 large peeled **shrimp**
7 oz **squid**, cleaned and
 cut into slices
small bunch of **parsley**,
 chopped
salt and **black pepper**

Heat the oil in a large shallow skillet, add the garlic and fennel, and cook for 8–10 minutes, until softened. Add the tomatoes, sherry, tomato paste, and 3 tablespoons of water and bring to a boil, then reduce the heat and simmer for 20 minutes.

Add the mussels, cover with a lid, and cook for 5–6 minutes, until the mussels have opened. Discard any that remain closed. Stir in the shrimp and squid and cook for another 3–4 minutes, until the shrimp turn pink and the squid is cooked through.

Sprinkle with parsley, season, and serve with crusty gluten-free bread, if desired.

For seafood salad, heat 2 tablespoons olive oil in a wok or skillet, add 2 chopped garlic cloves, and cook for 1 minute, then stir in 16 large peeled shrimp and 10 oz cleaned and sliced squid and stir-fry for 3–4 minutes, until the shrimp turn pink and the squid is cooked through. Toss with the leaves of 2 torn romaine lettuce and 1 cup snow peas. Serve with a squeeze of lime juice. **Calories per serving 165**

falafel burgers with avocado salsa

Calories per serving **299**
Serves **4**
Preparation time **15 minutes,
    plus chilling**
Cooking time **6–8 minutes**

1⅔ cups rinsed, drained
    canned **chickpeas**
2 **scallions**, chopped
2 **garlic cloves**, chopped
handful of **parsley**
1 teaspoon **ground cumin**
1 teaspoon **ground coriander**
½ teaspoon **harissa paste**
grated rind and juice of ½ **lime**
2 tablespoons **rice flour**
2 tablespoons **sunflower oil**
salt and **black pepper**
watercress, to serve

Salsa
4 ripe **tomatoes**, diced
1 **avocado**, peeled, pitted,
    and diced
½ small **red onion**, diced
1 tablespoon **extra virgin
    olive oil**
grated zest and juice of
    ½ **lime**

Put the chickpeas, scallions, garlic, parsley, spices, harissa, lime zest and juice, and flour into a blender or food processor. Season with salt and black pepper and process until fairly smooth. Using your hands, shape the mixture into 4 patties, then chill for 20 minutes.

Meanwhile, make the salsa. Mix together all the ingredients and set aside.

Heat the sunflower oil in a skillet and cook the patties for 3–4 minutes on each side, until lightly golden and heated through.

Serve with watercress and the salsa.

For avocado with hummus, put 1⅔ cups rinsed, drained canned chickpeas and 2 peeled garlic cloves into a food processor and pulse until broken down. Add 2 tablespoons tahini and the juice of 1 lime and process until smooth. With the motor still running, slowly pour in ½ cup olive oil until you have the consistency you like (a little water can be added to loosen, if needed). Peel and pit 2 avocados, then slice thickly and divide among 4 plates. Serve with the hummus and a squeeze of lemon juice, sprinkled with black pepper. **Calories per serving 468**

roasted cod with ratatouille

Calories per serving **269**
Serves **4**
Preparation time **10 minutes**
Cooking time **26–28 minutes**

400 g (13 oz) **zucchini**, sliced
2 **red bell peppers**, cored,
    seeded, and chopped
2 **red onions**, cut into wedges
1 **eggplant**, chopped
4 **garlic cloves**, sliced
2 tablespoons **olive oil**
2 cups **cherry tomatoes**
small handful of **basil leaves**,
    torn
4 **cod loins** (about 5 oz each)
salt and **black pepper**

Put the vegetables into a roasting pan and toss together with the garlic, oil, and salt and black pepper. Place in a preheated oven, at 425°F, for 16 minutes.

Add the tomatoes and basil to the vegetables and toss together. Nestle the cod loins among the vegetables, then return to the oven for another 10–12 minutes, or until the fish is cooked through.

For baked cod, tomatoes & leeks, put 4 cod loins (about 5 oz) into an aluminum foil-lined ovenproof dish. Drizzle with 2 tablespoons olive oil and the juice of 1 lemon, then add 2 trimmed, cleaned, and sliced leeks, 6 halved cherry tomatoes, and salt and black pepper. Toss together gently, then seal the foil to form a package. Place in a preheated oven, at 400°F, for 18–19 minutes, or until the fish is cooked through. Meanwhile, cook 4 peeled and chopped russet or Yukon Gold potatoes in a saucepan of boiling water for 12–15 minutes, until tender. Drain, then mash with 1 tablespoon plain yogurt, ½ tablespoon olive oil, and 4 sliced scallions. Serve the cod with the mashed potatoes. **Calories per serving 333**

quinoa & lamb stuffed bell peppers

Calories per serving **274**

Serves **4**

Preparation time **10 minutes**

Cooking time **35 minutes**

4 **red bell peppers**, halved, cored, and seeded

7 oz **ground lamb**

1 **garlic clove**, crushed

2 teaspoons **ground cumin**

1 teaspoon **paprika**

¼ cup **quinoa**

1 cup **gluten-free vegetable broth**

1 tablespoon chopped **mint**

1 tablespoon chopped **parsley**

steamed **green beans** and **zucchini**, to serve

Place the bell pepper halves, cut side up, in a roasting pan and roast in a preheated oven, at 400°F, for 20 minutes, until starting to soften.

Meanwhile, heat a nonstick skillet, add the ground lamb, and cook until it starts to brown. Stir in the garlic and spices and cook for 1 minute. Add the quinoa and broth, cover, and simmer for 10–12 minutes, until the quinoa is soft. Stir in the herbs.

Remove the roasted peppers from the oven and spoon in the lamb mixture, then return to the oven for another 15 minutes. Serve with steamed green beans and zucchini.

For lamb chops with peperonata, heat 1 tablespoon olive oil in a saucepan, add 1 large sliced onion, and sauté for 2–3 minutes. Add 2 cored, seeded, and sliced red bell peppers, 2 cored, seeded, and sliced yellow bell peppers, 2 sliced garlic cloves, and ½ teaspoon dried oregano and cook for 8–10 minutes, stirring frequently, until softened. Add 4 chopped plum tomatoes and cook for another 1–2 minutes. Stir in a few chopped basil leaves and season well. Meanwhile, broil 8 lamb cutlets until cooked to your preference. Serve with the peperonata and a squeeze of lemon juice. **Calories per serving 407**

oven-baked halibut

Calories per serving **227**
Serves **4**
Preparation time **15 minutes**
Cooking time **15 minutes**

4 **halibut fillets** (about
    5 oz each)
4 **tomatoes**, chopped
4 **scallions**, sliced
1 **red chile**, seeded and sliced
2 **garlic cloves**, sliced
2 **carrots**, peeled and cut into
    julienne strips
juice of 2 **limes**
2 tablespoons **gluten-free
    soy sauce**
few **cilantro** sprigs
salt and **black pepper**
steamed **green beans**,
    to serve

Place each halibut fillet on a large piece of nonstick parchment paper, then top each with one-quarter of the tomatoes and scallions. Divide the remaining ingredients among the fish and season with salt and black pepper.

Wrap up and seal the paper to form packages, then transfer to a baking sheet. Bake in a preheated oven, at 425°F), for 15 minutes, or until the fish is cooked through. Serve with steamed green beans.

For Thai-style halibut, heat 1 ½ teaspoons olive oil in a skillet, add 6 chopped scallions, and sauté for 1 minute, then stir in 2 tablespoons red Thai curry paste and cook for 1 minute. Stir in 1 cup gluten-free fish broth and 1⅔ cups coconut milk. Bring to a boil, then reduce the heat and simmer for 5 minutes. Add 4 halibut fillets (about 5 oz each), cover, and cook for 6–8 minutes, until the fish is cooked through. Divide 5 cups wilted spinach among 4 bowls, then spoon in the halibut and pour over the liquid. Serve sprinkled with 2 tablespoons toasted sesame seeds. **Calories per serving 427**

thai sesame chicken patties

Calories per serving **286**
Serves **4**
Preparation time **15 minutes, plus chilling**
Cooking time **10 minutes**

3 tablespoons **sesame seeds**
4 **scallions**
6 sprigs of **cilantro**, plus extra to garnish
1 lb **ground chicken**
1 tablespoon **gluten-free light soy sauce**
1½ inch piece of **fresh ginger root**, peeled and finely grated
1 **egg white**
1 tablespoon **sesame oil**
1 tablespoon **sunflower oil**
scallion curls, to garnish (optional)
½ cup **gluten-free Thai sweet chili dipping sauce**, to serve

Heat a nonstick skillet over medium-low heat and dry-fry the sesame seeds for 2 minutes, stirring frequently, until golden brown and toasted. Set aside.

Put the scallions and cilantro into a food processor and process until finely chopped. Alternatively, chop with a knife. Transfer to a bowl and mix with the chicken, toasted sesame seeds, soy sauce, ginger, and egg white.

Divide the mixture into 20 mounds on a cutting board, then, using wet hands, shape into slightly flattened patties. Chill for 1 hour (or longer if you have time).

Heat the sesame and sunflower oils in a large skillet, add the patties, and cook for 10 minutes, turning once or twice, until golden and cooked through to the center. Arrange on a serving plate and garnish with extra cilantro leaves and scallion curls, if desired. Serve with the chili dipping sauce.

For baby greens stir-fry, to serve as an accompaniment, heat 2 teaspoons sesame oil in the skillet, add 1 (8 oz) package prepared baby greens and baby vegetable stir-fry ingredients, and stir-fry for 2–3 minutes, until the vegetables are hot. Mix in 2 tablespoons gluten-free light soy sauce and 1 tablespoon gluten-free Thai sweet chili dipping sauce. **Calories per serving 54**

seared steak with creamy beans

Calories per serving **270**
Serves **4**
Preparation time **5 minutes**
Cooking time **20–25 minutes**

1 tablespoon **olive oil**
2 large **leeks**, trimmed,
   cleaned, and finely sliced
2 **garlic cloves**, finely chopped
1⅔ cups rinsed, drained
   canned **lima beans**
4 **tenderloin steaks**
   (about 5 oz each)
small bunch of **parsley**,
   chopped
1 tablespoon **plain yogurt**
2 tablespoons **extra virgin**
   olive oil
salt and **black pepper**

Heat the oil in a skillet, add the leeks and garlic, and sauté over low heat for 12–15 minutes, until soft. Add the beans and enough water just to cover, then simmer for 8–10 minutes, until the beans are soft.

Meanwhile, heat a ridged grill pan until hot and cook the steaks to your preference. Let rest.

Stir the parsley, yogurt, and olive oil into the beans and season with salt and black pepper.

Slice the steaks into large chunks and serve on a bed of creamy beans.

For spicy beans on toast, heat 1 tablespoon olive oil in a skillet, add 1 chopped leek and 1 cored, seeded, and chopped red bell pepper, and sauté for 5 minutes, until softened. Stir in 3¼ cups rinsed, drained canned lima beans, 2 tablespoons gluten-free ketchup, 1½ teaspoons gluten-free Worcestershire sauce, and 3 tablespoons water. Bring to a simmer and cook for 10–12 minutes. Season to taste, then add 2 tablespoons chopped parsley and 2 tablespoons slivered almonds. Toast 4 slices of gluten-free bread and spoon the beans over the toast to serve. **Calories per serving 310**

chicken with bell peppers

Calories per serving **241**
Serves **4**
Preparation time **10 minutes**
Cooking time **1 hour**

6 **tomatoes**, quartered
2 **red onions**, cut into thick
  wedges
1 **red bell pepper**, cored,
  seeded and chopped
1 **yellow pepper**, cored,
  seeded and chopped
4 **garlic cloves**, crushed
small bunch of **thyme**, leaves
  only
1 teaspoon **smoked paprika**
2 tablespoons **olive oil**
1 tablespoon **balsamic
  vinegar**
4 **boneless, skinless chicken
  thighs**, about 300 g (10 oz)
  in total
crisp green salad, to serve

Place all the ingredients except the chicken in a roasting pan and toss together, then top with the chicken.

Roast in a preheated oven, at 180°C (350°F), Gas Mark 4, for 1 hour, turning and basting occasionally, until the chicken is golden and cooked through. Serve with a crisp green salad.

For chicken & red pepper open sandwiches, spread 4 slices of gluten-free bread with 1 teaspoon pesto each. Top each one with 1 sliced, roasted red bell pepper, ½ sliced, cooked chicken breast, and a few arugula leaves. Sprinkle with black pepper and a drizzle of balsamic glaze, then serve immediately. **Calories per serving 266**

provençal fish stew

Calories per serving **234**
Serves **4**
Preparation time **15 minutes**
Cooking time **15–18 minutes**

1 tablespoon **olive oil**
3 **shallots**, thinly sliced
3 **garlic cloves**, chopped
1⅔ cups canned **diced tomatoes**
1 tablespoon **tomato paste**
1 **thyme sprig**
1¼ cups **gluten-free fish broth**
10 oz **fresh mussels**, scrubbed and debearded (discard any that don't shut when tapped)
1 lb **skinless cod** or **haddock fillet**, cut into pieces
7 oz **squid**, cleaned and sliced into rings
salt and **black pepper**
2 tablespoons chopped **parsley**, to garnish

Heat the oil in a large saucepan, add the shallots and garlic, and sauté for 3–4 minutes, until softened. Add the tomatoes, tomato paste, and thyme and cook for another 4–5 minutes.

Pour in the broth and bring to a boil, then add the mussels, fish, and squid, cover the pan, and cook for 5–6 minutes, until the mussels have opened and the fish is cooked through. Discard any mussels that remain closed.

Season with salt and black pepper, ladle into 4 bowls, and serve sprinkled with parsley.

For hot & sour fish soup, put 3½ cups hot, gluten-free fish broth, 1 teaspoon coriander seeds, and 1 inch piece of fresh ginger root, peeled and sliced, into a saucepan and simmer for 5 minutes. Add 1 tablespoon gluten-free Thai fish sauce, 2 thinly sliced red chiles, and 3 thinly sliced garlic cloves and simmer for another 2 minutes, then add 10 oz peeled jumbo shrimp and 7 oz skinless cod or haddock fillet, cut into pieces, and cook gently for 5–6 minutes, until the shrimp turn pink and the fish is cooked through. Add 2 sliced scallions and the juice of 1 lime. Season to taste and serve sprinkled with 2 tablespoons chopped cilantro. **Calories per serving 128**

eggplant casserole

Calories per serving **297**
  **(not including salad
  and bread)**
Serves **4**
Preparation time **10 minutes**
Cooking time **40–45 minutes**

2 **large eggplants**, sliced
2 tablespoons **olive oil**
1¼ cups coarsely chopped
  mozzarella cheese
¼ cup grated **Parmesan
  cheese**
salt and **black pepper**

Tomato sauce
1 tablespoon **olive oil**
1 **garlic clove**, crushed
1 small **onion**, finely chopped
1¾ cups canned **plum
  tomatoes**
handful of **basil**, torn

Make the tomato sauce. Heat the oil in a saucepan, add the garlic and onion, and sauté for 3–4 minutes, until softened. Add the tomatoes and basil, bring to a boil, then reduce the heat and simmer for 15 minutes.

Brush the eggplants with the oil on each side while the sauce is simmering. Heat a ridged grill pan until hot and cook the eggplant slices for 1–2 minutes on each side, until tender and browned.

Spoon a little of the tomato sauce into an ovenproof dish, layer over half the eggplants, sprinkle with half the mozzarella and Parmesan cheeses, and season well. Repeat the layering with the remaining ingredients, finishing with a sprinkling of the cheeses.

Put the casserole into a preheated oven, at 400°F, for 20–25 minutes, until golden and bubbling. Serve with salad and gluten-free crusty bread, if desired.

For spicy eggplant & chicken casserole, make the tomato sauce as above, adding 1 seeded and finely sliced red chile with the garlic and onion. Cook the eggplant and layer the casserole as above, interspersing 2 cups shredded, cooked chicken between the eggplant layers. Cook in the oven as above. **Calories per serving 382**

thai steamed fish

Calories per serving **210**
**(not including rice, bok
choy, and snow peas)**
Serves **4**
Preparation time **10 minutes**
Cooking time **10 minutes**

4 **trout fillets** (about 5 oz
each)
4 baby **bok choy**, quartered
lengthwise
2 inch piece of **fresh ginger
root**, peeled and sliced
2 **garlic cloves**, chopped
1 **red chile**, seeded and sliced
grated zest and juice of
2 **limes**
3 tablespoons **gluten-free
soy sauce**

Place the trout fillets and bok choy on 2 large pieces
of aluminum foil and sprinkle with the ginger, garlic,
chile, and lime zest and juice. Pour the soy sauce over
the top, then loosely seal the foil to form packages.

Transfer the packages to a steamer and cook for
10 minutes, or until the fish is cooked through.
Serve with lime halves jasmine rice and steamed bok
choy and snow peas, if desired.

For Thai fish soup, mix together 4¼ cups gluten-
free fish broth, 1½ tablespoons red Thai curry paste,
4 kaffir lime leaves, and 1 tablespoon gluten-free
Thai fish sauce in a saucepan. Bring to a simmer and
cook for 5 minutes, then add 10 oz skinless white fish
fillets, such as cod or halibut, and cook for 2 minutes.
Stir in 5 oz peeled jumbo shrimp, 3 baby bok choy,
quartered, and a handful of cilantro leaves and simmer
for 2–3 minutes, until the shrimp turn pink and the
fish is just cooked through. Serve immediately.
Calories per serving 148

mediterranean squid

Calories per serving **257**
Serves **4**
Preparation time **10 minutes**
Cooking time **25 minutes**

1 tablespoon **olive oil**
1 **red onion**, diced
1 **garlic clove**, sliced
¾ cup **pitted black ripe olives**
1 **red chile**, seeded and finely
  sliced
pinch of **paprika**
1⅔ cups canned **diced**
  tomatoes
1⅔ cups rinsed, drained
  canned **lima beans**
1¼ lb **squid**, cleaned and
  sliced into rings
grated zest of 1 **lemon**
small handful of **parsley**,
  chopped
salt and **black pepper**
lemon wedges, to serve

Heat the oil in a large saucepan, add the onion and garlic, and sauté for 3–4 minutes, until softened. Add the olives, chile, and paprika and cook for another 1 minute. Stir in the tomatoes and simmer for 12 minutes.

Add the lima beans and season well. Bring to a boil, then add the squid, cover, and simmer for 5–6 minutes, until the squid is cooked through and tender.

Sprinkle with the lemon zest and chopped parsley and serve with lemon wedges.

For battered squid, mix together 1 cup chickpea flour, ½ cup rice flour, 2 tablespoons crushed Sichuan peppercorns, 2 teaspoons cracked black pepper, and 1 teaspoon sea salt in a bowl. Heat about 3 inches vegetable oil in a deep saucepan or wok to 350–375°F, or until a cube of gluten-free bread browns in 30 seconds. Cut 13 oz cleaned squid into rings, then coat in the seasoned flour and deep-fry, in batches, for 2–3 minutes, until golden. Remove with a slotted spoon and drain on paper towels, sprinkling with a little more salt. Serve sprinkled with a few chopped scallions and a dipping sauce. **Calories per serving 232 (not including dipping sauce)**

chicken with mango salsa

Calories per serving **265**
Serves **4**
Preparation time **10 minutes**
Cooking time **6–8 minutes**

1 large **mango**, peeled, pitted,
  and diced
1 small **red onion**, diced
1 **red chile**, seeded and
  finely diced
large bunch of **parsley**,
  chopped
2 tablespoons **olive oil**
juice of ½ **lime**
4 **boneless, skinless chicken
  breasts** (about 5 oz each)
2 **garlic cloves**, halved
black pepper

Mix together the mango, red onion, chile, parsley,
1 tablespoon of the oil, and the lime juice in a bowl.
Set aside.

Place the chicken breasts between 2 sheets of
nonstick parchment paper or plastic wrap and flatten
with a rolling pin or mallet. Rub with the cut garlic,
sprinkle with black pepper, and drizzle with the
remaining oil.

Heat a large ridged grill pan over medium-high heat
and cook the chicken for 3–4 minutes on each side,
until cooked through. Serve with the salsa.

For chicken & mango toasts, spread 4 slices of
gluten-free whole-wheat bread with 1 tablespoon
gluten-free mango chutney each, then top each one
with 3–4 spinach leaves, a few cilantro leaves, and
⅓ cup sliced, cooked chicken. Sprinkle with ⅔ cup
shredded cheddar cheese and cook under a preheated
broiler for 3–4 minutes, until bubbling and golden.
Calories per serving 294

mini smoked trout quiches

Calories per serving **295**
Serves **4**
Preparation time **10 minutes**
Cooking time **12–15 minutes**

1 ½ teaspoons **canola oil**
13 cups **baby spinach leaves**
(about 13 oz)
6 **extra-large eggs**
½ cup **low-fat milk**
3 tablespoons grated
Parmesan cheese
2 tablespoons finely
chopped **chives**
5 oz **hot-smoked trout fillets**,
flaked
4 **cherry tomatoes**, halved
salt and **black pepper**

Line 8 cups of a muffin pan with 6 inch squares of wax paper.

Heat the oil in a skillet, add the spinach, and cook briefly until wilted. Remove from the heat.

Beat together the eggs, milk, and cheese in a small bowl and season to taste, then stir in the chives and trout.

Divide the spinach among the muffin liners, then pour in the egg mixture. Top each one with half a cherry tomato.

Bake the quiches in a preheated oven, at 350°F, for 12–15 minutes, until just set.

For smoked trout baked eggs, brush 4 ramekins with melted butter, then add 2 oz flaked hot-smoked trout fillet to each dish. Carefully break 2 eggs into each ramekin, top with 2 tablespoons shredded cheddar cheese, and season. Place the ramekins in a roasting pan with enough boiling water to come three-quarters of the way up the sides of the dishes. Bake in a preheated oven, at 400°F, for 8–9 minutes, until the cheese has melted and the egg is cooked but still soft. **Calories per serving 244**

vegetable & feta fritters

Calories per serving **207**
Serves **4**
Preparation time **10 minutes**
Cooking time **6–12 minutes**

1 **large zucchini**, grated
grated zest of **1 lemon**
2 **scallions**, sliced
2 tablespoons chopped
  parsley
2 tablespoons chopped **mint**
⅔ cup crumbled **feta cheese**
2 tablespoons **rice flour**
1 **egg yolk**
2 **cooked fresh beets**, peeled
  and grated
2 tablespoons **olive oil**
salt and **black pepper**
basil leaves, to garnish
mixed green salad, to serve

Mix together the zucchini, lemon zest, scallions, herbs, feta, rice flour, and egg yolk in a large bowl and season well. Gently stir in the beets until the mixture is just speckled with red.

Heat a little of the oil in a skillet, add tablespoons of the batter to the pan, and cook the fritters for 1–2 minutes on each side, until golden. Transfer to a serving plate and keep warm. Repeat with the remaining mixture, adding the remaining oil to the pan as necessary.

Garnish the fritters with basil leaves and serve with a mixed green salad.

For cucumber & yogurt dip, to serve as an accompaniment, mix together 1 cup fat-free Greek yogurt, 1 crushed garlic clove, 1 teaspoon toasted cumin seeds, ¼ grated cucumber, squeezed of excess liquid, and a pinch of paprika in a serving dish. Season well. **Calories per serving 33**

cheese & herb biscuits

Calories per biscuit **222**
**(not including butter
to serve)**
Makes **12**
Preparation time **15 minutes**
Cooking time **15 minutes**

2¼ cups **gluten-free all-
purpose flour**, plus extra
for dusting
1 tablespoon **gluten-free
baking powder**
1 teaspoon **dry mustard**
pinch of **cayenne pepper**
4 tablespoons **unsalted
butter**, diced
1¾ cups shredded **cheddar
cheese**
1 tablespoon chopped **chives**,
or herb of your choice
2 **extra-large eggs**
⅓ cup **buttermilk**

Sift the flour, baking powder, mustard, and cayenne
into a large bowl. Add the butter and rub in with the
fingertips until the mixture resembles bread crumbs.
Mix in 1½ cups of the shredded cheese and the herbs.

Beat the eggs with the buttermilk in a small bowl,
then mix into the flour to form a soft dough; do not
overwork the dough. Turn out onto a lightly floured
work surface and roll out to a thickness of 1 inch.
Stamp out 12 biscuits, using a 2 inch cutter, and
place on a baking sheet.

Sprinkle the remaining cheese over the biscuits and
bake in a preheated oven, at 425°F, for 15 minutes,
until risen and golden. Serve the biscuits warm, with
butter, if desired.

For cheese & herb muffins, mix together ⅔ cup
cornmeal, ¾ cup almond flour, ¾ cup tapioca (cassava)
flour, 1 tablespoon gluten-free baking powder,
¼ teaspoon paprika, 1 cup shredded cheddar cheese,
and 2 tablespoons chopped chives. Mix together ½ cup
sunflower oil, 2 eggs, and 1 cup milk, then mix the liquid
into dry ingredients to make a batter. Line a 12-cup
muffin pan with paper muffin liners and spoon in the
batter. Sprinkle each one with 2 teaspoons shredded
cheddar cheese and bake in a preheated oven, at
375°F, for 17–18 minutes, until golden. **Calories
per muffin 351**

cottage cheese & chive muffins

Calories per muffin **231**
Makes **12**
Preparation time **10 minutes**
Cooking time **30–35 minutes**

1 cup **cottage cheese**
⅔ cup **gluten-free all-purpose flour**
1½ cups **ground almonds (almond meal)**
⅔ cup drained, chopped **sun-dried tomatoes in oil**
2 teaspoons chopped **chives**
1 teaspoon **gluten-free baking powder**
1 cup grated **Parmesan cheese**
3 tablespoons **sunflower oil**
4 **extra-large eggs**, beaten
1 tablespoon **cold water**
salt and **black pepper**

Line a 12-cup muffin pan with paper muffin liners.

Put the cottage cheese, flour, ground almonds, tomatoes, chives, baking powder, and half of the cheese into a bowl. Add the oil, eggs, and measured water, season lightly, and gently mix together. Do not overmix.

Spoon the batter into the muffin liners and sprinkle with the remaining cheese. Bake in a preheated oven, at 400°F, for 30–35 minutes, until risen and golden. Serve warm.

For cottage cheese & chive snacks, mix together 1½ teaspoons cottage cheese, 2 tablespoons drained, chopped sun-dried tomatoes in oil, and 1 tablespoon chopped chives in a bowl. Divide the mixture between 12 gluten-free oat cakes or rice cakes, then sprinkle each one with ½ teaspoon grated Parmesan cheese and serve immediately. **Calories per snack 73**

lemon & raspberry cupcakes

Calories per cupcake **290**
Makes **12**
Preparation time **10 minutes**
Cooking time **12–15 minutes**

1¼ sticks **butter**, softened
¾ cup **sugar**
½ cup **rice flour**
⅔ cup **cornstarch**
1 tablespoon **gluten-free
  baking powder**
grated zest and juice of
  1 **lemon**
3 **eggs**, beaten
1 cup **raspberries**
1 tablespoon **gluten-free
  lemon curd**

Line a large 12-cup muffin pan with large paper muffin liners.

Whisk together all the ingredients except the raspberries and lemon curd in a large bowl. Fold in the raspberries.

Spoon half the sponge batter into the muffin liners, dot with a little of the lemon curd, then add the remaining sponge batter.

Bake the muffins in a preheated oven, at 400°F, for 12–15 minutes, until golden and firm to the touch. Remove from the oven, transfer to a wire rack, and let cool.

For citrusy muffins, make the sponge batter as above, adding the grated zest of 1 orange. Omit the raspberries and lemon curd and cook as above. Mix 1¼ cups confectioners' sugar and 1–2 teaspoons lemon juice in a bowl to make a fairly thick icing and drizzle it over the cooled muffins. Decorate with gluten-free lemon and orange jellies, if desired. **Calories per muffin 265 (not including candies)**

apricot & molasses oat squares

Calories per square **226**
Makes **12**
Preparation time **5 minutes**
Cooking time **25 minutes**

½ cup **coconut oil**, plus extra
  for greasing
¼ cup **black molasses**
1 tablespoon packed **dark
  brown sugar**
2½ tablespoons **light
  corn syrup**
2¾ cups **gluten-free
  rolled oats**
⅓ cup chopped **dried apricots**
⅓ cup **pumpkin seeds**
grated zest of **1 orange**

Grease a 7 inch square baking pan with coconut oil.

Melt together the coconut oil, molasses, sugar, and syrup in a large saucepan, stirring until the sugar has dissolved. Add the remaining ingredients and mix well. Spoon the batter into the prepared pan and level the top.

Bake the oat squares in a preheated oven, at 350°F, for 18–20 minutes, until golden. Let cool in the pan for 2 minutes before cutting into squares, then let cool completely in the pan. Store in an airtight container and eat within 5–6 days.

For spiced fruit oat squares, melt together the coconut oil and sugar with 1 tablespoon black molasses and ⅓ cup light corn syrup, stirring until the sugar has dissolved. Add 2¾ cups gluten-free rolled oats, 1 tablespoon golden raisins, 1 tablespoon candied peel, and 1 teaspoon ground cinnamon and mix well. Spoon into a 7 inch square baking pan and level the top. Bake and cut into squares as above. **Calories per square 198**

creamy mango smoothie

Calories per serving **282**
Serves **4**
Preparation time **10 minutes**

4 **ripe mangoes**, peeled
   and pitted
¼ cup **plain yogurt**
1 **banana**, chopped
4¼ cups **unsweetened**
   soy milk
2 teaspoons **honey** (optional)
ice cubes, to serve

Put all the ingredients except the honey and ice into a blender or food processor and blend until smooth. Taste for sweetness and add the honey, if required, then blend again.

Pour into 4 tall glasses and serve with ice cubes.

For marinated mango salad, toss together 4 peeled, pitted, and chopped mangoes, 2 oranges divided into sections, 1 cup blueberries, and 1 tablespoon shredded mint leaves in a nonmetallic bowl. Mix together 1 tablespoon honey, the grated zest and juice of 2 limes, and ¼ teaspoon ground cinnamon in a separate bowl. Pour the marinade over the mango salad and let marinate at room temperature for 25 minutes. Divide among 4 bowls and serve each with 1 tablespoon reduced-fat crème fraîche or plain Greek yogurt. **Calories per serving 287**

grilled bananas with blueberries

Calories per serving **258**
Serves **4**
Preparation time **5 minutes**
Cooking time **8–10 minutes**

4 **bananas**, unpeeled
½ cup **fat-free Greek yogurt**
¼ cup **gluten-free oatmeal**
   or **rolled oats**
1 cup **blueberries**
4 teaspoons **honey**, to serve

Heat a ridged grill pan over medium-high heat, add the bananas, and grill for 8–10 minutes, or until the skins are beginning to blacken, turning occasionally.

Transfer the bananas to 4 serving dishes and, using a sharp knife, cut open lengthwise. Spoon the yogurt over the fruit and sprinkle with the oatmeal or oats and blueberries. Serve immediately, drizzled with the honey.

For oatmeal, ginger & golden raisin yogurt, mix ½ teaspoon ground ginger with the yogurt in a bowl. Sprinkle with 2–4 tablespoons packed dark brown sugar, according to taste, the oatmeal, and ¼ cup golden raisins. Let stand for 5 minutes before serving. **Calories per serving 219**

spiced plum hazelnut meringue

Calories per serving **274**
Serves **8**
Preparation time **15 minutes,
  plus cooling**
Cooking time **2 hours**

5 **egg whites**
1 ¼ cups **superfine sugar**
⅔ cup **roasted hazelnuts,
  chopped**
8 **plums,** halved and pitted
½ teaspoon **allspice**
2 tablespoons packed
  dark brown sugar
juice of 1 **orange**
1 cup **fat-free Greek yogurt**

Line a baking sheet with nonstick parchment paper.

Whisk the egg whites in a large, clean bowl until stiff peaks form, then add 1 ½ teaspoons of the superfine sugar at a time, whisking well between each addition, until the mixture is thick and glossy. Fold in the hazelnuts.

Spoon the meringue onto the prepared baking sheet in large dollops that join up to make a circle. Make a shallow dip in the center with the back of a spoon.

Bake in a preheated oven, at 275°F, for 2 hours, until pale golden and crisp. Turn off the oven and let the meringue rest inside to cool completely.

Put the plums into a heatproof dish, cut side up, and sprinkle with the allspice, brown sugar, and orange juice. Cook under a preheated hot broiler until bubbling and golden. Let cool slightly.

Spoon the yogurt into the center of the meringue and spoon the plums over the top to serve.

For plum and crushed meringue desserts, halve, pit, and cut the plums into quarters, then put into a roasting pan and sprinkle with the allspice, dark brown sugar, and orange juice. Roast in a preheated oven, at 350°F, for 15–20 minutes, until tender. Let cool, then stir in 2 ½ cups fat-free Greek yogurt and 4 crushed prepared meringue nests. Divide among 8 bowls and serve sprinkled with 1 tablespoon chopped hazelnuts. **Calories per serving 109**

spiced baked pears

Calories per serving **218**
Serves **4**
Preparation time **10 minutes**
Cooking time **35–40 minutes**

4 **pears**, peeled, halved,
   and cored
½ cup **apple juice**
⅓ cup **maple syrup**
1 **vanilla bean**, split in half
   lengthwise
grated zest of 1 **lemon**
grated zest of 1 **orange**
5 **cardamom pods**, bruised
3 **star anise**
3 **cloves**
2 tablespoons **toasted
   slivered almonds**, to
   decorate
2 tablespoons **fat-free Greek
   yogurt**, to serve

Put the pears, cut side up, into an ovenproof dish.
Pour the apple juice and maple syrup over them, then
scrape the seeds on top from the vanilla bean. Sprinkle
with the grated citrus zest and spices. Cover with
aluminum foil.

Bake in a preheated oven, at 400°F, for 20 minutes,
then turn the pears over and cook, covered, for another
15–20 minutes, until tender.

Spoon the pears into 4 serving bowls, pour the juices
on top, and sprinkle with the almonds. Serve with
dollops of the yogurt.

For cinnamon oatmeal with grated pears, put
1½ cups gluten-free rolled oats and ½ teaspoon
ground cinnamon into a saucepan with 2½ cups low-
fat milk and cook over medium heat for 5–6 minutes,
stirring constantly, until thick and creamy. Pour into
4 bowls and grate 4 pears over the top. Serve with
a squeeze of lemon juice and sprinkling of ground
cinnamon. **Calories per serving 279**

yogurt & berry smoothie

Calories per serving **232**
Serves **4**
Preparation time **5 minutes**

1¼ cups **plain yogurt**
1 (1 lb) package **fresh** or
  frozen mixed berries,
  defrosted if frozen, plus
  extra to decorate
¼ cup **millet flakes**
3 tablespoons **honey**
1¼ cups **cranberry juice**

Put all the ingredients into a food processor or a blender and process until smooth.

Pour into 4 glasses, decorate with a few extra whole berries, and serve immediately.

For frozen raspberry yogurt slice, process 4 cups raspberries (about 1 lb), 1⅔ cups confectioners' sugar, the juice of 1 lemon, and 2½ cups fat-free Greek yogurt in a food processor or blender. Pour the mixture into a 9 x 5 x 3 inch loaf pan that has been lined with plastic wrap, then freeze until solid. Serve sliced with 2–2½ cups mixed berries. **Calories per serving 374**

lemon, pistachio & fruit squares

Calories per square **255**
Makes **15**
Preparation time **10 minutes,**
  plus chilling
Cooking time **20 minutes**

butter, for greasing
grated zest of 1 **lemon**
3 **dried dates,** chopped
½ cup plus 1 tablespoon
  chopped **unsalted**
  pistachio nuts
¾ cup **slivered almonds,**
  chopped
½ cup firmly packed **light**
  brown sugar
1½ cups **millet flakes**
1½ cups **gluten-free**
  cornflakes, lightly crushed
1⅓ cups canned **condensed**
  milk
3 tablespoons **mixed**
  pumpkin and sunflower
  seeds

Grease an 11 x 7 inch baking pan with butter.

Mix together all the ingredients in a large bowl until well combined and spoon the batter into the prepared pan.

Put into a preheated oven, at 350°F, for 20 minutes. Let cool in the pan, then mark into 15 squares and chill until firm. Store in an airtight container and eat within 3–5 days.

For chocolate fruit & nut squares, put 3 oz gluten-free white chocolate and 3 oz gluten-free semisweet chocolate in separate heatproof bowls set over saucepans of simmering water and let heat until melted. Drizzle the melted chocolates over the cooked and cooled squares and let set. **Calories per square 309**

142

less than
400 calories

avocado, bell pepper & olive salad

Calories per serving **342**
Serves **4**
Preparation time **10 minutes**
Cooking time **2 minutes**

1 tablespoon **sesame seeds**
2 **avocados**, peeled, pitted,
  and chopped
juice of 1 **lime**
1 **red bell pepper**, cored,
  seeded, and chopped
1 **yellow pepper**, cored,
  seeded, and chopped
½ **cucumber**, finely chopped
2 **carrots**, peeled and
  chopped
2 **tomatoes**, chopped
4 **scallions**, sliced
10 **pitted black ripe olives**,
  halved
1 **romaine lettuce**, coarsely
  torn
¼ cup **gluten-free French
  dressing**
1 tablespoon chopped **mint**

Heat a nonstick skillet over medium-low heat and dry-fry the sesame seeds for 2 minutes, stirring frequently, until golden brown and toasted. Set aside.

Meanwhile, put the avocados into a large bowl and toss with the lime juice to prevent discoloration. Gently toss together with the remaining ingredients except the sesame seeds.

Sprinkle the salad with the toasted sesame seeds and serve.

For peperonata with avocado & olives, heat 3 tablespoons olive oil in a skillet, add 2 sliced garlic cloves and 3 sliced onions, and cook for 1–2 minutes. Core, seed, and slice 2 red bell peppers and 2 yellow bell peppers, then add to the pan and cook for 10 minutes. Add 3 chopped ripe tomatoes and cook for another 12–15 minutes, until the bell peppers are soft. Stir in 1 peeled, pitted, and chopped avocado, 12 halved pitted black ripe olives, and a small handful of basil leaves. Serve with gluten-free crusty bread, if desired. **Calories per serving 307 (not including bread)**

roasted butternut & cashew soup

Calories per serving **317**
Serves **4**
Preparation time **10 minutes**
Cooking time **25 minutes**

1 **butternut squash** (about
　2 lb), peeled, seeded, and
　chopped into ½ inch chunks
2 tablespoons **olive oil**
1 tablespoon chopped **sage**
2 tablespoons **pumpkin
　seeds**
1 **onion**, chopped
1 **garlic clove**, chopped
½ tablespoon **mild curry
　powder**
2 tablespoons **cashew nuts**
2½ cups hot **gluten-free
　vegetable broth**
½ cup **plain yogurt**
salt and **black pepper**

Put the squash into a roasting pan and toss with
1 tablespoon of the oil and the sage. Place in a
preheated oven, at 425°F, for 18–20 minutes, until
tender and golden.

Meanwhile, heat a nonstick skillet over medium-low
heat and dry-fry the pumpkin seeds for 2–3 minutes,
stirring frequently, until golden brown and toasted.
Set aside.

Heat the remaining oil in a saucepan, add the onion
and garlic, and sauté for 4–5 minutes, until softened.
Stir in the curry powder and cook for another
minute, stirring.

Add the roasted squash, cashews, and broth and
bring to a boil, then reduce the heat and simmer for
3–4 minutes. Stir in the yogurt. Using a handheld
blender, blend the soup until smooth. Season to taste.

Ladle the soup into 4 bowls and serve sprinkled with
the toasted pumpkin seeds.

For mashed squash & potatoes with cabbage,
cook 1 peeled, seeded, and chopped butternut squash
(about 1¾ lb) and 3 peeled and chopped potatoes in
a saucepan of boiling water for 12–15 minutes, until
tender. Meanwhile, cook ½ shredded savoy cabbage
in a separate saucepan of boiling water for 4–5 minutes,
then drain and keep warm. Meanwhile, poach 4 eggs
(see page 32). Drain the squash and potatoes, then
mash in the pan with 1 tablespoon plain yogurt,
1 tablespoon chopped sage, and 2 tablespoons butter.
Season well and stir in the cabbage. Serve topped with
the poached eggs. **Calories per serving 300**

gingered cauliflower soup

Calories per serving **347**
Serves **6**
Preparation time **15 minutes**
Cooking time **25 minutes**

1 tablespoon **sunflower oil**
2 tablespoons **butter**
1 **onion**, coarsely chopped
1 head of **cauliflower**, cut
   into florets, core discarded
   (about 3¾ cups prepared)
1½ inch piece of **fresh ginger**
   root, peeled and finely
   chopped
3¾ cups **gluten-free**
   vegetable or **chicken broth**
1¼ cups **low-fat milk**
⅔ cup **heavy cream**
salt and **black pepper**

Soy-glazed seeds
1 tablespoon **sunflower oil**
2 tablespoons **sesame seeds**
2 tablespoons **sunflower**
   seeds
2 tablespoons **pumpkin seeds**
1 tablespoon **gluten-free**
   soy sauce

Heat the oil and butter in a saucepan, add the onion, and sauté for 5 minutes, until softened but not browned. Stir in the cauliflower florets and ginger, then the broth. Season with salt and black pepper and bring to a boil. Cover and simmer for 15 minutes, until the cauliflower is just tender.

Meanwhile, make the glazed seeds. Heat the oil in a skillet, add the seeds, and cook for 2–3 minutes, stirring until lightly browned. Add the soy sauce, then quickly cover the pan with a lid until the seeds have stopped popping. Set aside.

Puree the cooked soup, in batches, in a blender or food processor, then pour back into the saucepan and stir in the milk and half the cream. Bring just to a boil, then taste and adjust the seasoning, if needed.

Ladle the soup into 6 shallow bowls, drizzle with the remaining cream, and sprinkle with some of the glazed seeds, serving the remaining seeds in a small bowl for additional sprinkling.

For creamy cauliflower & cashew soup, heat the oil and butter as above, then add the chopped onion and ½ cup cashew nuts and sauté until the onions are softened and the nuts lightly browned. Mix in the cauliflower florets and broth as above, then season with salt, black pepper, and a little grated nutmeg. Simmer for 15 minutes. Meanwhile, sauté ½ cup cashew nuts in 1 tablespoon butter until pale golden, add 1 tablespoon honey, and cook for 1–2 minutes, until golden and caramelized. Puree the soup and finish with milk and cream as above, ladle into 6 bowls, and garnish with the cashew nuts. **Calories per serving 340**

spicy shrimp tacos

Calories per serving **365**

Serves **4**

Preparation time **10 minutes, plus marinating**

Cooking time **3 minutes**

1 tablespoon **olive oil**

juice of 1 **lime**

2 **garlic cloves**, peeled and crushed

½ **red chile**, seeded and finely chopped

13 oz **peeled jumbo shrimp**

8 **gluten-free corn taco shells**

1 **romaine lettuce**, shredded

¾ cup **prepared guacamole**

¾ cup **prepared salsa**

Mix together the oil, lime juice, garlic, and chile in a nonmetallic dish, then stir in the shrimp. Let marinate for 20 minutes.

Heat the tacos according to the package directions.

Meanwhile, heat a nonstick skillet, add the shrimp, and cook for 2–3 minutes, until the shrimp turn pink and are cooked through.

Stuff the tacos with shredded lettuce, then top with the shrimp, guacamole, and salsa and serve immediately.

For spicy shrimp soup, pour 3¾ cups gluten-free fish broth into a saucepan, add 2 chopped red chiles, 2 crushed garlic cloves, 1 crushed lemon grass stalk, and a ¾ inch piece of fresh ginger root, peeled and sliced, and simmer for 15 minutes. Add 10 oz peeled jumbo shrimp and 3 sliced scallions and cook for 2–3 minutes, until the shrimp turn pink and are just cooked through, then stir in 2 chopped bok choy, a small bunch each of chopped mint and cilantro, and ½ cup bean sprouts. Cook for another 3–4 minutes, then squeeze in the juice of ½ lime and serve. **Calories per serving 101**

chicken balti with whole spices

Calories per serving **320**
(not including rice)
Serves **4**
Preparation time **20 minutes**
Cooking time **40 minutes**

1 **onion**, quartered
1 inch piece of **fresh ginger
root**, peeled and sliced
3 **garlic cloves**
2 tablespoons **sunflower oil**
8 **boneless, skinless chicken
thighs** (about 1¼ lb in total),
cubed
1 teaspoon **cumin seeds**,
coarsely crushed
1 **cinnamon stick**, halved
8 **cardamom pods**, coarsely
crushed
6 **cloves**
½ teaspoon **turmeric**
1 teaspoon **dried red
pepper flakes**
1⅔ cups canned **diced
tomatoes**
2½ cups **gluten-free
chicken broth**
small bunch of **cilantro**, torn
¼ cup **toasted slivered
almonds**, to garnish

Put the onion, ginger, and garlic into a food processor
and process until finely chopped. Alternatively, chop
with a knife.

Heat the oil in a medium saucepan, add the chicken,
and cook, stirring, for 5 minutes, until lightly browned.
Stir in the chopped onion and ginger mixture and cook
for 2–3 minutes, until softened.

Stir in the spices and red pepper flakes and cook for
1 minute, then mix in the tomatoes and broth. Bring
to a boil, then reduce the heat, cover, and simmer
for 30 minutes, stirring occasionally, until the chicken
is cooked through.

Add the cilantro and cook for 1 minute, then spoon into
4 bowls. Sprinkle with the almonds and serve with rice,
if desired.

For chicken balti with mushrooms & spinach, omit
the cumin seeds, cardamom, cloves, turmeric, and red
pepper flakes and stir in 2 tablespoons gluten-free,
medium-hot Indian curry paste instead. Mix in 2 cups
sliced cup mushrooms and cook as above. Stir in
5 cups baby spinach leaves along with the cilantro
at the end and cook until the spinach has just wilted.
Calories per serving 324

paneer & bell pepper tikka masala

Calories per serving **398**
(not including rice)
Serves **4**
Preparation time **10 minutes**
Cooking time **20–25 minutes**

1 ½ teaspoons **sunflower oil**
7 ½ oz **paneer cheese**, cubed
2 **red bell peppers**, cored,
seeded, and chopped
2 **yellow bell peppers**, cored,
seeded, and chopped
2 baby **bok choy**, quartered
¼ cup **gluten-free tikka
masala curry paste**
⅔ cup **reduced-fat crème
fraîche** or **plain Greek
yogurt**
2 tablespoons chopped
cilantro leaves

Heat the oil in a wok or skillet, add the paneer, and cook for 4–5 minutes, until golden. Remove with a slotted spoon and drain on paper towels.

Add the bell peppers and bok choy to the pan and stir-fry for 4–5 minutes, until starting to soften. Stir in the curry paste, add ¼ cup of water, and cook for another 8–10 minutes.

Stir in the crème fraîche and simmer for 2 minutes, then return the paneer to the pan with the cilantro and simmer for 2–3 minutes, until heated through. Serve with basmati rice, if desired.

For paneer-stuffed bell peppers, heat 1 tablespoon olive oil in a skillet, add ¼ teaspoon mustard seeds, ½ teaspoon turmeric, 1 teaspoon cumin seeds, and ½ teaspoon paprika, and cook until the mustard seeds start to pop. Add 7 ½ oz cubed paneer and cook for 3–4 minutes, until golden. Stir in ⅔ cup frozen peas and 1 diced tomato and cook for 1 minute. Cut 2 romano peppers in half, remove the seeds, and spoon the paneer mixture into each half. Place on a baking sheet and roast in a preheated oven, at 400°F, for 10–12 minutes, until the peppers have softened. **Calories per serving 270**

chicken salad wraps

Calories per serving **321**
Serves **4**
Preparation time **10 minutes**

4 **gluten-free prepared
tortillas**
¼ cup **gluten-free reduced-
fat mayonnaise**
4 teaspoons **gluten-free
mango chutney**
2 **carrots**, peeled and grated
2 **cooked chicken breasts**,
shredded
¼ small **cabbage**, thinly
shredded
2 **tomatoes**, sliced
small handful of **cilantro
leaves**
salt and **black pepper**

Lay the tortillas on a clean surface and spread each one
with 1 tablespoon of the mayonnaise and 1 tablespoon
of the mango chutney.

Divide the remaining ingredients among the tortillas
and season with salt and black pepper. Roll up the
wraps to serve.

For chicken club sandwiches, cook 8 bacon strips
under a preheated hot broiler for 3–4 minutes on
each side until crisp. Toast 12 slices of gluten-free
bread for 2–3 minutes on each side. Spread 4 slices
of the toast with 2 tablespoons gluten-free reduced-
fat mayonnaise. Top the slices with some shredded
iceberg lettuce, 3 sliced tomatoes, and the bacon.
Spread another 4 slices of toast with 2 tablespoons
gluten-free mango chutney and place on top of the
bacon. Cover the mango with 2 sliced cooked chicken
breasts and 1 thinly sliced small red onion. Top with the
remaining slices of toast and secure each sandwich
with 2 toothpicks. Slice in half diagonally to serve.
Calories per serving 457

beef olives

Calories per serving **340**
Serves **4**
Preparation time **15 minutes**
Cooking time **2¼ hours**

1 tablespoon **olive oil**
2 **onions**, chopped
4 **mushrooms**, chopped
2 **bacon strips**, chopped
1 **garlic clove**, chopped
1 teaspoon **thyme leaves**,
   chopped
4 **bottom round roast** or
   rump roast steaks (about
   5 oz each)
1 tablespoon **gluten-free
   Dijon mustard**
2 **carrots**, peeled and diced
2 **celery sticks**, diced
1⅔ cups **gluten-free
   beef broth**
1 cup **red wine**
steamed **cabbage** and
   carrots, to serve

Heat half the oil in a skillet, then add half the onion, the mushrooms, bacon, and garlic and sauté for 3–4 minutes, until softened. Stir in the thyme leaves.

Spread each steak with one-quarter of the mustard, then divide the stuffing mixture among them, roll up, and secure with kitchen twine.

Heat the remaining oil in a flameproof casserole or Dutch oven and brown the beef rolls on all sides, then remove from the dish and set aside. Add the remaining onion, the carrots, and celery to the dish and cook for 3–4 minutes, then return the beef to the dish with the broth and wine. Bring to a simmer, cover, and cook over low heat for 2 hours.

Serve with steamed cabbage and carrots.

For serious beef sandwiches, cut 2 red onions into wedges, then toss with 1 tablespoon olive oil and 1 teaspoon cumin seeds. Put into a roasting pan and roast in a preheated oven, at 400°F, for 20–25 minutes, until starting to char at the edges. Cook 4 sirloin steaks (about 5 oz each) in a hot ridged grill pan until cooked to your preference. Spread 4 thick slices of gluten-free bread with 1 teaspoon gluten-free horseradish sauce each. Top each one with a small handful of arugula leaves. Place the steaks on top, then divide the roasted red onion wedges between them and top with another 4 slices of bread. Serve with homemade fries, if desired. **Calories per serving 465 (not including fries)**

teriyaki chicken salad

Calories per serving **320**
Serves **4**
Preparation time **20 minutes,
    plus marinating**
Cooking time **20–25 minutes**

4 **boneless, skinless chicken
    breasts** (about 4 oz each)
2 tablespoons **sunflower oil**
¼ cup **gluten-free soy sauce**
2 **garlic cloves**, finely chopped
1 inch piece of **fresh ginger
    root**, peeled and finely
    grated
2 tablespoons **sesame seeds**
2 tablespoons **sunflower
    seeds**
2 tablespoons **pumpkin
    seeds**
juice of 2 **limes**
3½ cups **herb salad**
½ small **iceberg lettuce**,
    torn into bite-size pieces
1½ cups **alfalfa sprouts**

Put the chicken breasts into a shallow, nonmetallic dish. Spoon three-quarters of the oil over the chicken, then add half the soy sauce, the garlic, and ginger. Turn the chicken to coat in the mixture, cover with plastic wrap, and let marinate in the refrigerator for 30 minutes.

Heat a nonstick skillet until hot. Lift the chicken out of the marinade, add to the pan, and cook for 8–10 minutes on each side, until browned and cooked through. Remove from the pan and set aside.

Heat the remaining oil in the pan, add the seeds, and cook for 2–3 minutes, until lightly toasted. Add the remaining marinade and soy sauce and bring to a boil, then remove from the heat and mix in the lime juice.

Mix the herb salad, lettuce, and sprouts together, then divide among 4 serving plates. Thinly slice the chicken and arrange on top. Spoon the seed dressing on top and serve immediately.

For teriyaki chicken with Asian salad, marinate the chicken as above and make a salad with 3 carrots, cut into thin strips, 4 scallions, cut into thin strips, 6 thinly sliced radishes, and ½ small head of Chinese greens, thinly shredded. Cook the chicken as above, omit the seeds, and then continue with the dressing as above. Slice the chicken, arrange on the salad, and drizzle with the warm dressing. **Calories per serving 239**

potato pancakes

Calories per serving **399**
Serves **4**
Preparation time **10 minutes**
Cooking time **20–25 minutes**

4 **russet** or **Yukon Gold**
   potatoes, peeled and
   chopped
1 ½ teaspoons **gluten-free**
   baking powder
2 **eggs**
¼–⅓ cup **skim milk**
1 tablespoon **sunflower oil**
salt and **black pepper**

To serve
4 **eggs**
8 **bacon strips**

Cook the potatoes in a saucepan of boiling water for 12–15 minutes, until tender. Drain, then return to the pan and mash until smooth. Beat in the baking powder, eggs, and enough of the milk to form a smooth batter the consistency of thick cream. Season well.

Heat the oil in a skillet and drop in tablespoonfuls of the batter. Cook for 3–4 minutes, turning once, until golden brown. Remove from the pan and keep warm. Repeat with the remaining batter.

Meanwhile, bring a saucepan of water to a gentle simmer and stir with a large spoon to create a swirl. Break 2 eggs into the water and cook for 3–4 minutes. Remove with a slotted spoon and keep warm. Repeat with the remaining eggs.

Cook the bacon under a preheated hot broiler for 5–6 minutes, or until crisp.

Serve the potato pancakes with the bacon and poached eggs.

baked sole with fennel pesto

Calories per serving **370**
Serves **4**
Preparation time **20 minutes**
Cooking time **15 minutes**

1 **fennel bulb**, coarsely
    chopped
2 tablespoons chopped **dill**
⅓ cup **pine nuts**, toasted
2 tablespoons **ground
    almonds (almond meal)**
½ cup grated **Parmesan
    cheese**
juice of ½ **lemon**
½ cup **olive oil**, plus
    1 tablespoon for drizzling
4 **lemon sole** or **flounder
    fillets** (about 6 oz each),
    skinned
2 **zucchini**
2 cups **green beans**
2 **tomatoes**, chopped

Put the fennel into a blender or food processor and blend to a puree. Add the dill, pine nuts, ground almonds, cheese, and lemon juice and process to combine. With the motor still running, slowly pour in the ½ cup olive oil through the feed tube until combined.

Lay the fish fillets on a board, skinned side up, and spread with the fennel pesto. Using a vegetable peeler, slice the zucchini into long, thin strips, then put 2–3 slices onto each sole fillet. Roll up the fish and place in an ovenproof dish.

Drizzle with the remaining oil, cover with aluminum foil, and bake in a preheated oven, at 375°F, for 15 minutes, until cooked through.

Meanwhile, cook the green beans in a steamer, then toss with the tomatoes and divide among 4 plates. Top each with a fish fillet and serve.

For sole & fennel soup, heat 1 tablespoon olive oil in a large saucepan, add 1 chopped onion and 2 sliced garlic cloves, and cook for 2 minutes, until starting to soften. Add 2 thinly sliced fennel bulbs and cook for another 8 minutes. Stir in ½ cup white wine and cook for 2 minutes, then add 2 cups hot gluten-free fish broth, 3⅓ cups canned diced tomatoes, and salt and black pepper. Bring to a boil, then reduce the heat and simmer for 5 minutes. Add 1¼ lb chopped skinned sole or flounder fillets and cook for 3 minutes, or until cooked through. Stir in 2 tablespoons chopped parsley and serve with gluten-free crusty bread. **Calories per serving 245 (not including bread)**

mushroom chili

Calories per serving **347**
Serves **4**
Preparation time **10 minutes**
Cooking time **15–20 minutes**

1 tablespoon **olive oil**
1 **onion**, diced
2 **red chiles**, seeded and
  finely diced
1 **garlic clove**, crushed
2 teaspoons **ground cumin**
13 oz **mixed mushrooms**,
  chopped
1⅔ cups canned **diced
  tomatoes**
1 tablespoon **tomato paste**
1⅔ cups rinsed, drained
  canned **red kidney beans**
2–3 tablespoons **water**
2 tablespoons chopped
  parsley
salt and **black pepper**
3 cups cooked **basmati rice**,
  to serve

Heat the oil in a skillet, add the onion, and sauté for 2–3 minutes, until starting to soften. Stir in the chiles, garlic, and cumin and cook for another 2 minutes.

Add the mushrooms, tomatoes, tomato paste, kidney beans, and measured water, bring to a simmer, and cook for 12–15 minutes.

Season to taste and stir in the chopped parsley, then serve with the cooked basmati rice.

For garlic mushrooms on toast, heat 1 tablespoon olive oil in a skillet, add 5 cups sliced cremini mushrooms, and sauté for 4–5 minutes, until softened. Add 2 finely chopped garlic cloves and cook for 1 minute, then stir in 2 tablespoons crème fraîche or plain Greek yogurt. Meanwhile, toast 4 thick slices of gluten-free bread. Season the mushrooms to taste and spoon them on top of the toast. Serve sprinkled with 1 tablespoon chopped parsley. **Calories per serving 200**

pork, apple & ginger stir-fry

Calories per serving **357**
Serves **4**
Preparation time **15 minutes**
Cooking time **12–15 minutes**

2 tablespoons **sesame seeds**
1 tablespoon **coconut oil**
10 oz **pork tenderloin**, cut
   into strips
2 **garlic cloves**, chopped
2 inch piece of **fresh ginger
   root**, peeled and cut into
   matchsticks
1 **green chile**, seeded and
   chopped
2 **apples**, cored and cut into
   wedges
2 **carrots**, peeled and cut
   into matchsticks
2 cups **broccoli florets**
10 oz **thick rice noodles**
juice of 1 **lime**

Heat a nonstick skillet over medium-low heat and dry-fry the sesame seeds for 2 minutes, stirring frequently, until golden and toasted. Set aside.

Heat the oil in a wok or large skillet, add the pork, and stir-fry for 6–8 minutes, until lightly browned. Add the garlic, ginger, chile, apples, and vegetables and stir-fry for another 4–5 minutes, or until the pork is cooked through.

Meanwhile, cook the noodles according to the package directions, then add to the stir-fry with the lime juice and toss all the ingredients together.

Serve sprinkled with the toasted sesame seeds.

For broiled pork cutlets with apple & ginger coleslaw, cook 4 pork cutlets (about 5 oz each) under a preheated hot broiler for 3–4 minutes on each side, or until cooked through. Meanwhile, finely slice 1 small green cabbage, 2 celery sticks, and 1 cored and seeded red bell pepper and put into a bowl. Add 2 peeled and grated carrots and 2 peeled, cored, and grated apples and mix well. Mix together 2 tablespoons plain yogurt, a 1 inch piece of fresh ginger root, peeled and grated, and 1 tablespoon gluten-free mayonnaise in a small bowl, then stir into the coleslaw with 2 tablespoons chopped cilantro. Serve with the broiled pork. **Calories per serving 386**

roasted veggie & quinoa salad

Calories per serving **372**
Serves **4**
Preparation time **5 minutes**
Cooking time **20–25 minutes**

3 **zucchini**, cut into chunks
2 **red bell peppers**, cored,
   seeded, and cut into chunks
2 **red onions**, cut into wedges
1 **large eggplant**, cut into
   chunks
3 **garlic cloves**, peeled
3 tablespoons **olive oil**
1 cup **quinoa**
2 tablespoons **green pesto**
   or **tomato paste**
1 tablespoon **balsamic
   vinegar**
3 cups **arugula leaves**

Put all the vegetables and garlic onto a large baking sheet and drizzle over the olive oil. Place in a preheated oven, at 425°F, for 20–25 minutes, until tender and beginning to char.

Meanwhile, cook the quinoa in a saucepan of boiling water according to the package directions, then drain well.

Whisk together the pesto or tomato paste and balsamic vinegar in a small bowl. Put the roasted vegetables, arugula, and quinoa into a large serving bowl and stir in the dressing. Serve warm.

For quinoa with salmon & watercress, cook the quinoa as above. Meanwhile, place 2 large pieces of skinless salmon fillet (about 10 oz in total) in a nonstick skillet and cook for 3 minutes on each side until crisp and just cooked through, then flake. Whisk together 1 cup light crème fraîche or plain Greek yogurt, the grated zest and juice of 1 orange, and 1 tablespoon gluten-free whole-grain mustard in a small bowl. Stir the dressing into the quinoa with the flaked salmon and a bunch of chopped watercress. **Calories per serving 381**

mackerel curry

Calories per serving **381**
Serves **4**
Preparation time **10 minutes**
Cooking time **15–20 minutes**

1 **green chile**, seeded
   and chopped
1 teaspoon **ground coriander**
½ teaspoon **turmeric**
4 **garlic cloves**
1 inch piece of **fresh ginger
   root**, peeled and sliced
1 teaspoon **sunflower oil**
1 tablespoon **coconut oil**
1 teaspoon **cumin seeds**
1 large **onion**, sliced
⅔ cup **coconut milk**
1 cup **water**
14½ oz **mackerel fillets**,
   cut into 2 inch pieces
small handful of **cilantro
   leaves**, coarsely torn
salt and **black pepper**

Put the chile, ground coriander, turmeric, garlic, ginger, and sunflower oil into a blender or food processor and blend together to make a smooth paste.

Heat the coconut oil in a wok or skillet over medium heat, add the spice paste and the cumin seeds, and cook for 2–3 minutes.

Add the onion to the pan and cook for 1–2 minutes, then pour in the coconut milk and measured water. Bring to a boil, then reduce the heat and simmer for 5 minutes. Season with salt and black pepper.

Add the mackerel pieces to the pan and cook for 6–8 minutes, until the fish is cooked through, then stir in the cilantro leaves.

For mackerel, beet & horseradish salad, cut 5 raw beets (about 15 oz) into 4–6 wedges, put into a roasting pan with 2 tablespoons olive oil, 2 teaspoons cumin seeds, 2 tablespoons thyme, and 2 teaspoons honey, and mix to coat. Roast in a preheated oven, at 400°F, for 25 minutes, until tender. Meanwhile, whisk together 2 tablespoons gluten-free creamed horseradish, ¼ cup lemon juice, and ⅔ cup low-fat plain yogurt in a small bowl. Heat 4 smoked mackerel fillets (about 3 oz each) according to the package directions, then flake into large flakes. Put a few small handfuls of baby spinach leaves onto 4 plates and sprinkle with the mackerel and beets. Sprinkle with the horseradish dressing and serve. **Calories per serving 412**

granola

Calories per serving **305**
Serves **4**
Preparation time **5 minutes,
    plus cooling**
Cooking time **20 minutes**

1 ½ teaspoons **sunflower oil**
1 tablespoon **maple syrup**
1 ½ teaspoons **honey**
1 cup **gluten-free rolled oats**
1 ½ tablespoons **sunflower
    seeds**
1 tablespoon **sesame seeds**
1 ½ tablespoons **pumpkin
    seeds**
¼ cup **slivered almonds**
3 tablespoons **dried
    cranberries**
3 ½ tablespoons **unsweetened
    dried coconut**

To serve
1 ⅔ cups **plain yogurt**
2 cups hulled, halved
    strawberries (about 11 oz)

Mix together the oil, maple syrup, and honey in a bowl,
then add the oats, seeds, and almonds and mix well.

Spread the mixture over a baking sheet and bake
in a preheated oven, at 250°F, for 10 minutes. Stir in
the cranberries and coconut, then return to the oven
and cook for another 10 minutes; keep an eye on the
mixture, because nuts and seeds can burn easily.

Spoon onto a tray and let cool, then divide among
4 bowls and serve with the yogurt and strawberries.

For bircher muesli, mix together 1 cup gluten-free
rolled oats, ⅓ cup apple juice, a large pinch each of
ground cinnamon and nutmeg, 1 grated sweet, crisp
apple, 1 tablespoon chopped pecans, 1 tablespoon
dried cranberries, and ⅔ cup water in a large bowl.
Cover and let soak overnight in the refrigerator. Stir
in 2 tablespoons low-fat plain yogurt, divide among
4 bowls and serve sprinkled with 2 tablespoons fresh
raspberries. **Calories per serving 211**

blueberry pancakes

Calories per serving **363**
Serves **4**
Preparation time **5 minutes**
Cooking time **10–15 minutes**

1 **gluten-free all-purpose
   flour**
2 teaspoons **gluten-free
   baking powder**
1 **egg**
²⁄₃ cup **soy milk**
2 tablespoons **unsalted
   butter**, melted
²⁄₃ cup **blueberries**
1 tablespoon **olive oil**

To serve
¼ cup **crème fraîche** or
   plain Greek yogurt
¼ cup **maple syrup**

Mix together the flour and baking powder in a large
bowl. Whisk together the egg and milk in a small bowl,
then pour into the dry ingredients and whisk until
smooth. Whisk in the melted butter, then stir in ½ cup
of the blueberries.

Heat the oil in a skillet over medium heat, then spoon
tablespoonfuls of the batter into the pan. Cook for
3–4 minutes, until golden underneath, then flip the
pancakes over and cook for another 2–3 minutes.
Remove from the pan and keep warm. Repeat with
the remaining batter.

Serve with the remaining blueberries, dollops of crème
fraîche, and a drizzle of maple syrup.

For blueberry smoothies, put 3 cups apple juice,
1²⁄₃ cups plain yogurt, 3 chopped bananas, and
3½ cups blueberries into a blender or food processor
and blend until smooth, adding a little milk if too thick.
Pour into 4 glasses to serve. **Calories per serving 258**

sweet french toast with berries

Calories per serving **370**
Serves **4**
Preparation time **15 minutes**
Cooking time **4–6 minutes**

2 **oranges**
1⅔ cups **fat-free Greek yogurt**
⅔ cup **blueberries**
⅔ cup hulled, quartered **strawberries**
2 **eggs**, beaten
¼ cup **sugar**
2 tablespoons **sesame seeds**
pinch of **ground cinnamon**
2 tablespoons **unsalted butter**
4 slices of **gluten-free bread**

Grate the zest of the oranges, then stir into the yogurt and chill. Separate the oranges into sections over a bowl to catch the juice.

Put the blueberries and strawberries into bowl. Add the orange sections and pour the juice over the fruit.

Whisk together the eggs, sugar, sesame seeds, and ground cinnamon in a shallow bowl.

Melt the butter in a large skillet over medium heat. Dip the slices of bread into the egg mixture, then transfer to the pan and cook for 2–3 minutes on each side until golden.

Serve each slice of French toast topped with one-quarter of the fruit and a dollop of the yogurt, with the juices poured over the top.

For warm berry compote & yogurt, put 1 cup raspberries, ¾ cup blueberries, and 1¼ cups hulled, halved strawberries into a small saucepan with 2 tablespoons honey and heat through for 6–7 minutes, stirring occasionally. Divide 2 cups fat-free Greek yogurt among 4 small bowls or glasses and pour the warm compote over the top. Serve immediately. **Calories per serving 145**

hazelnut, chocolate & pear cake

Calories per serving **319**
**(not including crème
fraîche)**
Serves **8**
Preparation time **20 minutes,
plus cooling**
Cooking time **45 minutes**

6 tablespoons **butter**, diced,
plus extra for greasing
3 oz **gluten-free semisweet
chocolate**, broken into
pieces
1 tablespoon **Amaretto liqueur**
3 **eggs**, separated
1/3 cup **superfine** or
granulated sugar
2/3 cup **hazelnuts**, toasted
and ground
3 **pears**, peeled, halved,
and cored
confectioners' sugar,
for dusting

Grease a 10 inch loose-bottom cake pan with butter
and line the bottom with nonstick parchment paper.

Melt the butter and chocolate in a heatproof bowl set
over a saucepan of gently simmering water, making
sure the bottom of the bowl does not touch the water.
Remove from the heat, stir in the Amaretto, and let cool.

Whisk the egg yolks and sugar into a bowl until pale
and thick. Fold into the chocolate mixture with the
ground hazelnuts. Whisk the egg whites in a separate
clean bowl until soft peaks form, then carefully fold
2 tablespoons of the mixture into the chocolate mixture.
Repeat until all the whites are folded in.

Spoon the batter into the prepared pan and level
the top. Arrange the pear halves over the batter, cut
side down.

Bake in a preheated oven, at 350°F, for 40 minutes,
until the pears are soft and the cake is cooked through.
Let cool slightly in the pan, then turn out onto a wire
rack and let cool completely.

Dust with confectioners' sugar and serve with low-fat
crème fraîche, if desired.

chocolate cake

Calories per serving **392**
Serves **6**
Preparation time **5 minutes**
Cooking time **35–40 minutes**

⅓ cup **coconut oil**, melted,
plus extra for greasing
1⅔ cups rinsed, drained
canned **kidney beans**
⅔ cup **rice flour**
½ cup plus 1 tablespoon
**gluten-free unsweetened
cocoa powder**, plus extra
for sifting
1½ teaspoons **gluten-free
baking powder**
½ cup firmly packed **light
brown sugar**
3 **extra-large eggs**
raspberries, to serve

Grease an 8 inch spring-form cake pan with coconut oil and line the bottom with nonstick parchment paper.

Put all the ingredients into a food processor or blender and process to a smooth batter, then spoon the batter into the prepared pan.

Bake the cake in a preheated oven, at 350°F, for 35–40 minutes, until a toothpick inserted into the center comes out clean. Let cool slightly in the pan, then turn out onto a wire rack and let cool completely before serving.

Sift with cocoa powder and serve with a few raspberries.

For chocolate mousse, melt 7½ oz chopped gluten-free semisweet chocolate in a heatproof bowl set over a saucepan of gently simmering water, making sure the bottom of the bowl does not touch the water. Add 2 teaspoons butter, 1 tablespoon brandy (optional), and 3 extra-large egg yolks, one at a time, stirring until combined. Let cool slightly. Whisk 3 egg whites in a large, clean bowl until just stiff. In a separate bowl, beat ⅔ cup heavy cream until lightly whipped, then fold the cream and egg whites into the chocolate mixture. Spoon into 6 small glasses or ramekins and chill for at least 1 hour before serving. **Calories per serving 383**

caramelized mixed fruits

Calories per serving **309**
Serves **4**
Preparation time **10 minutes**
Cooking time **15–20 minutes**

4 tablespoons **butter**
¼ cup **sugar**
juice of **1 orange**
3 **crisp, sweet apples**, peeled,
    cored, and quartered
3 **pears**, peeled, cored, and
    quartered
4 **plums**, halved and pitted

Heat the butter in a large skillet, add the sugar and orange juice, and cook, stirring, until the sugar dissolves. Increase the heat and cook for 6–8 minutes, until the mixture turns golden.

Add the apples and pears and stir into the caramel. Cook for 4–5 minutes, until they start to soften.

Stir in the plums and cook for another 4–5 minutes, until all the fruit is soft and coated in caramel. Serve warm.

For mixed fruit compote, put 2 cored and sliced apples, 2 cored and sliced pears, 4 halved and pitted plums, 6 dried apricots, 6 pitted prunes, the juice of 2 oranges, 2 tablespoons honey, 3 cloves, and 1 cinnamon stick in a large saucepan and bring to a boil, then reduce the heat and simmer for 8–9 minutes. Spoon into 4 bowls and top each with 3 tablespoons plain Greek yogurt. Serve sprinkled with ground nutmeg.
Calories per serving 246

blackberry & apple crisps

Calories per serving **358**
Serves **4**
Preparation time **10 minutes**
Cooking time **22–25 minutes**

4 **sweet, crisp apples**, peeled,
  cored, and thinly sliced
1 cup **blackberries**
2 teaspoons **granulated**
  sugar
1¼ cups **gluten-free**
  rolled oats
4 tablespoons **unsalted**
  butter, diced
3 tablespoons packed
  dark brown sugar
¼ cup **slivered almonds**

Divide the apple slices and blackberries among
4 small ovenproof dishes or ramekins and sprinkle
with the granulated sugar.

Put the oats, butter, brown sugar, and almonds into a
food processor and process until the mixture resembles
bread crumbs. Spoon the oat mixture over the fruit.

Bake the dessert in a preheated oven, at 375°F, for
22–25 minutes, until golden.

For blackberry & apple whip, whip 1¼ cups
heavy cream until soft peaks form. Gently fold in
3 unsweetened stewed apples and 1 cup lightly
crushed blackberries. Divide among 4 glasses and
chill until ready to serve. **Calories per serving 416**

berry & fromage frais whip

Calories per serving **313**
Serves **4**
Preparation time **5 minutes,**
   plus cooling and chilling
Cooking time **5 minutes**

3 tablespoons **crème de**
   cassis or **spiced red**
   fruit syrup
2 cups **mixed frozen berries**
2–4 tablespoons
   confectioners' sugar
2 cups **fat-free fromage**
   frais, **quark**, or **plain**
   Greek yogurt
1 cup **low-fat black currant**
   or **blueberry yogurt**
1 **vanilla bean**, split in half
   lengthwise
¼ cup **toasted slivered**
   almonds, to serve

Put the crème de cassis or syrup into a saucepan over low heat and gently heat, then add the berries. Stir, cover, and cook for about 5 minutes, or until the fruit has defrosted and is beginning to collapse. Remove from the heat and stir in 1–3 tablespoons of the confectioners' sugar, according to taste. Cool completely, then chill for at least 1 hour.

Mix together the fromage frais, yogurt, and remaining 1 tablespoon of confectioners' sugar in a bowl. Scrape in the seeds from the vanilla bean and beat to combine.

Fold the berries into the creamy mixture until just combined. Carefully spoon into 4 decorative glasses or glass serving dishes and serve immediately, sprinkled with the toasted almonds.

For exotic fruit whip, replace the crème de cassis with 3 tablespoons unsweetened coconut cream and the mixed berries with 8 oz exotic fruit mix and add 1 tablespoon lime juice. Heat as above, then blend in a food processor or blender until smooth. Chill as above. Mix the fromage frais with 2 tablespoons unsweetened coconut cream and 1 cup low-fat mango yogurt instead of the black currant yogurt. Fold in the fruit puree and serve sprinkled with ¼ cup toasted coconut flakes.
Calories per serving 313

less than
500 calories

broiled salmon with kale salad

Calories per serving **463**
Serves **4**
Preparation time **15 minutes**
Cooking time **8–11 minutes**

1 tablespoon **sunflower seeds**
3 cups shredded **kale**
4 **salmon fillets** (about 5 oz each)
¼ small **red cabbage**, shredded
1 **carrot**, peeled and cut into matchsticks
1 **avocado**, peeled, pitted, and sliced
6 **cherry tomatoes**, halved
2 tablespoons **extra virgin olive oil**
juice of ½ **lime**
½ teaspoon **gluten-free Dijon mustard**
½ teaspoon **maple syrup**
2 tablespoons chopped **chives**
black pepper

Heat a nonstick skillet over medium-low heat and dry-fry the sunflower seeds for 2–3 minutes, stirring frequently, until slightly golden and toasted. Set aside.

Put the kale into a colander, then pour over boiling water to slightly wilt the kale. Refresh under cold running water and drain.

Cook the salmon fillets under a preheated hot broiler for 3–4 minutes on each side, or until cooked through.

Meanwhile, toss the kale together with the cabbage, carrot, avocado, and tomatoes in a serving bowl. Whisk together the remaining ingredients and pour the dressing over the salad.

Sprinkle the toasted seeds over the salad. Serve the salad with the salmon, seasoned with black pepper.

For Chinese-style kale with pan-fried tuna, heat

1 tablespoon sunflower oil in a wok and stir-fry 2 sliced garlic cloves for a few seconds, then add 3 cups shredded kale. Toss around in the garlicky oil, then pour in ½ cup boiling water and cook for 5–6 minutes, until the kale has wilted. Meanwhile, heat 1 tablespoon olive oil in a separate skillet and cook 4 tuna steaks (about 5 oz each) for 3–4 minutes on each side, depending on how rare you prefer your tuna. Stir 1 tablespoon gluten-free soy sauce and 1 tablespoon gluten-free oyster sauce into the kale and heat through. Serve topped with the tuna.
Calories per serving 288

orange & shrimp noodle salad

Calories per serving **459**
Serves **4**
Preparation time **10 minutes**
Cooking time **5 minutes**

2 tablespoons **sesame seeds**
10 oz **rice noodles**
2 **oranges**
10 oz **cooked, peeled
jumbo shrimp**
1 bunch of **watercress** or
3½ cups of other **peppery
greens**
1 **red onion**, finely sliced
3 tablespoons **gluten-free
sweet chili dipping sauce**
juice of 1 **lime**
2 **Bibb**, **Boston**, or other small
butterhead lettuce, leaves
separated

Heat a nonstick skillet over medium-low heat and dry-fry the sesame seeds for 2 minutes, stirring frequently, until golden brown and toasted. Set aside.

Cook the rice noodles according to the package directions, then refresh under cold running water.

Separate the oranges into sections over a bowl to catch the juice. Transfer the noodles to a large bowl, add the orange sections, shrimp, watercress, and onion, and mix together.

Add the sweet chili sauce and lime juice to the orange juice and whisk together. Pour the dressing over the noodle mixture and toss together.

Arrange the lettuce leaves on a large serving plate or 4 individual plates and top with the noodle salad. Sprinkle with the toasted sesame seeds and serve.

For shrimp cocktail, mix together the grated zest of 1 orange, ¼ cup gluten-free mayonnaise, and 1 tablespoon gluten-free ketchup in a small bowl. Shred ½ small iceberg lettuce and divide among 4 glass bowls. Top with 13 oz cooked, peeled shrimp, then pour the mayonnaise dressing on top. Serve sprinkled with 1 tablespoon toasted slivered almonds and 1 tablespoon chopped cilantro. **Calories per serving 237**

smoked mackerel superfood salad

Calories per serving **492**
Serves **4**
Preparation time **15 minutes**
Cooking time **20 minutes**

½ **butternut squash**, peeled,
   seeded, and cut into ½ inch
   cubes
3 tablespoons **olive oil**
1 teaspoon **cumin seeds**
1 head of **broccoli**, cut into
   florets
1⅓ cups **frozen** or **fresh peas**
3 tablespoons **quinoa**
3 tablespoons **mixed seeds**
2 **smoked mackerel fillets**
juice of 1 **lemon**
½ teaspoon **honey**
½ teaspoon **gluten-free
   Dijon mustard**
1 cup shredded **red cabbage**
4 **tomatoes**, chopped
4 **cooked fresh beets**,
   cut into wedges
⅔ cup **radish sprouts**

Put the squash into a roasting pan and sprinkle with 1 tablespoon of the oil and the cumin seeds. Put into a preheated oven, at 400°F, for 15–18 minutes, until tender. Let cool slightly.

Meanwhile, cook the broccoli in a saucepan of boiling water for 4–5 minutes, until tender, adding the peas 3 minutes before the end of the cooking time. Remove with a slotted spoon and refresh under cold running water, then drain. Cook the quinoa in the broccoli water for 15 minutes, or according to the package directions, then drain and let cool slightly.

Heat a nonstick skillet over medium-low heat and dry-fry the seeds, stirring frequently, until golden brown. Set aside. Heat the mackerel fillets according to the package directions, then skin and break into flakes.

Whisk together the remaining oil, lemon juice, honey, and mustard in a small bowl. Toss together all the ingredients, except the radish sprouts, with the dressing in a serving bowl. Serve topped with the sprouts.

For smoked mackerel superfood soup, heat 1 tablespoon oil in a saucepan and sauté 1 chopped onion and 1 crushed garlic clove for 3–4 minutes. Add 4½ cups peeled, seeded, and diced butternut squash, 1½ cups broccoli florets, 2 tablespoons quinoa, 2½ cups gluten-free vegetable broth, and ⅔ cup orange juice and simmer for 15 minutes. Blend until smooth. Stir in 2 skinned, flaked smoked mackerel fillets and cook for 1 minute. Serve sprinkled with 2 tablespoons toasted pumpkin seeds. **Calories per serving 416**

parsnip, lentil & walnut salad

Calories per serving **435**
Serves **4**
Preparation time **10 minutes**
Cooking time **30–35 minutes**

4 **parsnips**, peeled and
   cut into batons
¼ cup **olive oil**
¼ cup **walnuts**
3 cups **gluten-free**
   vegetable broth
1 cup **green lentils**
juice of ½ **lemon**
1 teaspoon **honey**
½ teaspoon **gluten-free**
   whole-grain mustard
½ **garlic clove**, crushed
10 sprigs of **watercress** or
   1 cup of other **peppery**
   greens
1 cup **arugula leaves**
1 cup **baby spinach leaves**
3 tablespoons **Parmesan**
   cheese shavings

Put the parsnips into a roasting pan and drizzle with
1 tablespoon of the oil. Roast in a preheated oven, at
400°F, for 30–35 minutes, until golden, adding the
walnuts 5 minutes before the end of the cooking time.

Meanwhile, bring the broth to a boil in a saucepan,
add the lentils, and cook for 25–30 minutes, or
according to the package directions, until the lentils
are just tender. Drain.

Whisk together the remaining oil, lemon juice, honey,
mustard, and garlic in a small bowl.

Transfer the lentils, walnuts, and parsnips to a serving
bowl, then toss together with the dressing and salad
greens. Serve topped with Parmesan shavings.

For curried parsnip & lentil soup, heat 1 tablespoon
olive oil in a saucepan, add 3 peeled and chopped
parsnips, and cook for 2–3 minutes. Stir in 1 teaspoon
curry powder and ¼ cup red lentils and cook for
1 minute, then stir in 3¾ cups gluten-free vegetable
broth. Simmer for 20–25 minutes, until the parsnips
are tender. Remove from the heat and blend with
a handhand blender, adding a little milk to loosen
if needed. Ladle into 4 bowls and serve sprinkled
with 1 tablespoon chopped toasted walnuts and
½ tablespoon grated Parmesan cheese. **Calories
per serving 198**

spicy tomato tagliatelle

Calories per serving **442**
Serves **4**
Preparation time **5 minutes**
Cooking time **10 minutes**

1 ½ teaspoons **olive oil**
1 **red chile**, seeded and diced
2 inch piece of **fresh ginger root**, peeled and grated
3 **garlic cloves**, finely sliced
1 ⅔ cups canned **diced tomatoes**
1 teaspoon **sugar**
3–4 **anchovy fillets** in oil, drained
2 tablespoons chopped **parsley**
13 oz **gluten-free dried tagliatelle**
salt and **black pepper**
2 tablespoons shredded **cheddar cheese**, to serve

Heat the oil in a skillet, add the chile and ginger, and cook for 1 minute, then add the garlic and cook for another 1 minute.

Pour in the tomatoes, stir in the sugar and anchovies, and bring to a simmer. Cook for 5–6 minutes. Add the parsley and season to taste.

Meanwhile, cook the tagliatelle in a saucepan of boiling water according to the package directions. Drain and return to the pan, then pour in the sauce and toss together well.

Serve sprinkled with the shredded cheese.

For spicy tomato soup, heat 1 tablespoon olive oil in a saucepan, add 2 chopped onions, 1 peeled and chopped carrot, and 3 cored, seeded, and chopped red bell peppers, and cook for 10–12 minutes, until softened. Add 3 sliced garlic cloves and 1 sliced red chile and cook for another 2–3 minutes. Pour in 1 ⅔ cups canned diced tomatoes and 3 ½ cups gluten-free vegetable broth and bring to a boil, then reduce the heat and simmer for 10–15 minutes. Blend using a handhand blender, then season. Ladle into 4 bowls and serve with a drizzle of olive oil and sprinkling of black pepper. **Calories per serving 163**

shrimp & spinach curry

Calories per serving **474**
Serves **4**
Preparation time **10 minutes**
Cooking time **12–15 minutes**

4 **tomatoes**
2 tablespoons **peanut oil**
2 **red onions**, chopped
1 inch piece of **fresh ginger
    root**, peeled and grated
4 **garlic cloves**, sliced
¼ teaspoon **chili powder**
½ teaspoon **turmeric**
1 teaspoon **ground coriander**
1⅔ cups **reduced-fat
    coconut milk**
3 cups chopped **spinach**
14 oz **peeled jumbo shrimp**
1 tablespoon **toasted
    slivered almonds**
3 cups **cooked basmati**
    or other **long-grain rice**,
    to serve

Put the tomatoes into a heatproof bowl and pour over enough boiling water to cover. Let stand for 1–2 minutes, then drain, cut a cross at the stem end of each tomato, peel off the skins, and chop.

Heat the oil in a wok or large skillet, add the onions, ginger, and garlic, and stir-fry for 2–3 minutes. Add the spices and cook for another 2–3 minutes, then add the tomatoes. Pour in the coconut milk and bring to a simmer. Gradually add the spinach, stirring until wilted. Cook for 4–5 minutes.

Stir in the shrimp and cook for another 2 minutes, or until the shrimp turn pink and are cooked through. Sprinkle with the almonds and serve with the cooked rice.

For shrimp & spinach souffles, heat 1 tablespoon olive oil in a saucepan, add 7½ cups baby spinach, and cook for 2–3 minutes, until wilted. Meanwhile, melt 3 tablespoons butter in a saucepan, then stir in ¼ cup gluten-free all-pupose flour to make a roux. Gradually whisk in 1½ cups milk and cook, stirring continuously, for 2–3 minutes, until the sauce is thick and smooth. Stir in ⅔ cup grated Parmesan cheese, season, and pour into a large bowl. Stir in the spinach and let cool for 3–4 minutes. Put 3 cooked, peeled jumbo shrimp in each of 4 greased ramekins, then place on a baking sheet. Whisk 4 egg yolks into the spinach sauce. Whisk 4 egg whites in a large, clean bowl until stiff, then gently fold into the spinach mixture. Spoon into the ramekins, running a finger around the rim to help even rising. Sprinkle with 2 tablespoons grated Parmesan cheese and bake in a preheated oven, at 400°F, for 20 minutes, until risen and golden. **Calories per serving 386**

roasted salmon & vegetables

Calories per serving **457**
Serves **4**
Preparation time **15 minutes**
Cooking time **40–45 minutes**

3 **sweet potatoes** (about
  1 ¼ lb), peeled and cut
  into wedges
1 large **fennel bulb**, cut into
  8 wedges
2 **garlic cloves**, chopped
small bunch of **parsley**,
  chopped
2 tablespoons **olive oil**
1 tablespoon chopped **mint**
4 **salmon fillets** (about 4 oz
  each), skin scored 3 times
grated zest and juice of
  1 **lemon**
black pepper

To serve
¼ cup **Parmesan cheese**
  shavings
lemon wedges

Cook the sweet potatoes and fennel in a saucepan of boiling water for 4 minutes, then drain. Transfer to a roasting pan and sprinkle with the garlic, half the parsley, the olive oil, and black pepper. Toss together. Roast in a preheated oven, at 425°F, for 20–25 minutes, until the vegetables are tender and golden.

Meanwhile, rub the remaining parsley and the mint into the scored salmon skin. Set aside.

Lay the salmon, skin side up, on top of the vegetables, sprinkle with the lemon zest and juice and roast for another 15 minutes, or until the fish is cooked through and the vegetables are tender.

Sprinkle with the Parmesan shavings and serve with lemon wedges.

For fennel & salmon soup, heat 1 tablespoon olive oil in a saucepan, add 2 chopped shallots, and sauté for 2–3 minutes. Add 13 oz new potatoes and 2 chopped fennel bulbs and cook for another 3–4 minutes. Pour in 3¾ cups gluten-free vegetable broth and simmer for 10–12 minutes, until the vegetables are tender. Blend with a handhand blender, then return to the heat, season, and drop in 13 oz skinless salmon fillet, cut into chunks, and cook for 3–4 minutes, until the fish is cooked through. Ladle into 4 bowls and serve sprinkled with chopped parsley.
Calories per serving 325

beet & goat cheese risotto

Calories per serving **451**
Serves **4**
Preparation time **10 minutes**
Cooking time **25 minutes**

1½ teaspoons **olive oil**
1 large **onion**, chopped
4¼ cups **gluten-free
  vegetable broth**
½ cup **water**
8 **cooked fresh beets**,
  coarsely grated
2 **garlic cloves**, peeled
  and chopped
1½ cups **risotto rice**
½ cup **red wine**
1 tablespoon grated
  Parmesan cheese
2 tablespoons chopped **dill**
3 oz **goat cheese**, chopped
salt and **black pepper**

Heat the oil in a saucepan, add the onion, and sauté
for 5 minutes, until softened.

Meanwhile, pour the broth and measured water into a
separate saucepan, add half the beets, and gently heat.

Add the garlic to the onion and cook for another
1 minute, then stir in the rice. Pour in the wine and
let it sizzle. When the liquid is reduced, add a ladle of
the hot beet broth and stir. Continue to cook and stir
until the liquid has been absorbed, then repeat with
another ladle of broth. Continue cooking until almost
all of the broth is used and the rice is al dente.

Stir in the remaining grated beets and cook, stirring,
until the risotto is creamy.

Add the Parmesan and dill, season to taste, then divide
among 4 bowls. Top with the goat cheese and serve.

For beet & goat cheese salad, cook 4 raw beets in
a saucepan of salted boiling water for 30–40 minutes,
until tender. Drain, then peel off the skins. Cut each
beet into wedges and toss in a salad bowl with 8 oz
goat cheese, crumbled, ¾ bunch of watercress
or 3 cups of other peppery greens, 3 tarragon
sprigs, leaves stripped and torn, ¼ sliced cucumber,
2 tablespoons balsamic vinegar, and 2 tablespoons
extra virgin olive oil. Serve sprinkled with 2 tablespoons
toasted pumpkin seeds and black pepper. **Calories
per serving 342**

chicken with spinach & ricotta

Calories per serving **441**
Serves **4**
Preparation time **10 minutes**
Cooking time **25 minutes**

4 **boneless, skinless chicken**
breasts (about 4 oz each)
½ cup crumbled **ricotta**
cheese
⅔ cup cooked **spinach**,
squeezed dry
¼ teaspoon **grated nutmeg**
8 slices of **prosciutto**
2 tablespoons **olive oil**,
plus extra for drizzling
salt and **black pepper**

To serve
lemon wedges
arugula leaves

Make a long horizontal slit through the thickest part of each chicken breast without cutting right through.

Chop the spinach and mix with the ricotta and nutmeg in a bowl. Season with salt and black pepper.

Divide the stuffing among the slits in the chicken breasts and wrap each one in 2 pieces of prosciutto, winding it around the chicken to cover the meat totally.

Heat the oil in a shallow ovenproof pan, add the chicken breasts, and cook for 4 minutes on each side, or until the ham starts to brown. Transfer to a preheated oven, at 400°F, and cook for 15 minutes, until the chicken is cooked through. Serve with lemon wedges and arugula leaves drizzled with olive oil.

For chicken with mozzarella & sun-dried tomatoes,
omit the ricotta, spinach and nutmeg, and stuff each chicken breast with a slice of mozzarella cheese (about 6 oz total) and a drained piece of sun-dried tomato. Season well with black pepper and continue as above.
Calories per serving **471**

butternut & coconut curry

Calories per serving **470**
Serves **4**
Preparation time **10 minutes**
Cooking time **30 minutes**

1 tablespoon **vegetable oil**
1 large **onion**, sliced
2 **green chiles**, seeded
  and sliced
½ cup peeled and grated
  fresh ginger root
4 teaspoons **Thai curry paste**
2 **garlic cloves**, crushed
3⅓ cups **low-fat coconut milk**
½ **butternut squash**, peeled,
  seeded, and cut into
  bite-size pieces
½ cup **red lentils**
7 cups **baby spinach leaves**
bunch of **cilantro**, chopped
2 cups **cooked basmati**
  or other **long-grain rice**,
  to serve

Heat the oil in a saucepan, add the onion, and sauté for 3–4 minutes, until softened, then add the chiles, ginger, curry paste, and garlic and cook, stirring, for another 2 minutes.

Pour in the coconut milk and bring to a boil, then add the squash. Reduce the heat and simmer for 12 minutes, then stir in the lentils and simmer for another 10 minutes, until the squash is tender and the lentils have softened.

Stir in the spinach leaves and cilantro and cook for 2 minutes, until wilted. Serve with the cooked rice.

For roasted butternut & lentil salad, toss 5 cups chopped butternut squash and 2 red onions, cut into wedges, with 1 tablespoon olive oil, 1 crushed garlic clove, and 2 teaspoons thyme leaves. Roast in a preheated oven, at 400°F, for 25–30 minutes, until tender. Meanwhile, whisk together 1 tablespoon balsamic vinegar, 1 tablespoon olive oil, and 1 teaspoon gluten-free whole-grain mustard in a small bowl. Put 4 cups cooked, cooled green lentils into a serving bowl, add 8–10 halved cherry tomatoes and 3½ cups baby spinach leaves, then toss with the dressing. Add the roasted vegetables, toss again, and serve sprinkled with ⅔ cup crumbled feta cheese. **Calories per serving 376**

sausage & bean stew

Calories per serving **472**
Serves **4**
Preparation time **10 minutes**
Cooking time **20–25 minutes**

1 tablespoon **olive oil**
1 **onion**, chopped
2 **garlic cloves**, crushed
2 **carrots**, peeled and diced
4 good-quality **gluten-free sausages**
2 cups **gluten-free chicken broth**
1½ cups canned **cherry tomatoes**
1⅔ cups rinsed, drained canned **lima beans**
3 cups thickly shredded **savoy cabbage**
large bunch of **parsley**, chopped
salt and **black pepper**
4 cups **mashed potatoes**, to serve

Heat the oil in a large flameproof casserole or Dutch oven, add the onion, and sauté for 4–5 minutes, until softened, then add the garlic and carrots and cook for another 2–3 minutes.

Add the sausages and cook for 6–8 minutes, turning occasionally, until just golden.

Pour in the broth, tomatoes, beans, cabbage, and half the chopped parsley and simmer for 6–8 minutes, until the sausages are cooked through and the cabbage is tender. Season to taste and sprinkle with the remaining parsley. Serve with the mashed potatoes.

For sausage & bean breakfast, chop the sausages into bite-size pieces and cook in a skillet with 1½ teaspoons olive oil for 5–6 minutes, until browned. Add the lima beans and cherry tomatoes, season, and simmer for 10–12 minutes. Stir in 1 tablespoon chopped parsley, then make 4 dips in the mixture. Break 1 egg into each dip and cook for 6–8 minutes, until the sausages and eggs are cooked through. (If you prefer your eggs cooked more, finish by placing the dish under the broiler before serving.) **Calories per serving 309**

nasi goreng

Calories per serving **447**
Serves **4**
Preparation time **15 minutes**
Cooking time **10 minutes**

2 **extra-large eggs**
3 tablespoons **sunflower oil**
1 tablespoon **tomato paste**
1 tablespoon **gluten-free
    ketjap manis** (sweet dark
    soy sauce)
3 cups **cooked rice**
1 tablespoon **gluten-free
    light soy sauce**
2 inch piece of **cucumber,**
    quartered lengthwise and
    sliced
8 **scallions**, thinly sliced on
    the diagonal
salt and **black pepper**

Spice paste
2 tablespoons **vegetable oil**
4 **garlic cloves,** coarsely
    chopped
⅓ cup coarsely chopped
    shallots
3 tablespoons **roasted
    salted peanuts**
6 **medium-hot red chiles,**
    seeded and chopped
1 teaspoon **salt**

Make the spice paste. Put all of the ingredients into
a blender or food processor and process to a smooth
paste, or grind using a mortar and pestle.

Beat the eggs and season. Heat 1 tablespoon of
the sunflower oil in a small skillet over medium-high
heat, pour in one-third of the beaten egg, and cook
until set on top. Flip, cook for a few more seconds,
then turn out and roll up tightly. Repeat two times
with the remaining egg. Slice the omelets across
into thin strips.

Heat a wok over high heat until smoking. Add
2 tablespoons of the oil and the spice paste and
stir-fry for 1–2 minutes. Add the tomato paste
and ketjap manis and cook for a few seconds,
then add the cooked rice and stir-fry over high
heat for 2 minutes, until heated through.

Add the strips of omelet and stir-fry for another
1 minute, then add the soy sauce, cucumber, and
most of the scallions and toss together well. Spoon
into 4 bowls, sprinkle with the remaining scallions,
and serve.

For quick spicy rice broth, put 2 cups cooked rice
into a saucepan with 1 cup coconut milk, 2½ cups
hot gluten-free vegetable broth, 2 tablespoons tomato
paste, and 1 tablespoon mild curry powder. Bring to a
boil and cook over high heat for 4–5 minutes. Remove
from the heat and stir in 6 finely shredded scallions
and ¼ cucumber, finely shredded. Season, ladle into
4 bowls, and serve. **Calories per serving 245**

turkey chili

Calories per serving **499**
Serves **4**
Preparation time **15 minutes**
Cooking time 1¾ **hours**

1 tablespoon **olive oil**
2 **red onions**, chopped
1 **carrot**, peeled and diced
1 **celery stick**, diced
1 **red bell pepper**, cored,
   seeded, and chopped
1 **yellow bell pepper**, cored,
   seeded, and chopped
1 **red chile**, seeded and
   finely chopped
1 teaspoon **smoked paprika**
1 teaspoon **ground cumin**
bunch of **cilantro**, coarsely
   chopped
3 cups coarsely chopped or
   shredded **cooked turkey**
1⅔ cups rinsed, drained
   canned **lima beans**
3⅓ cups canned **diced
   tomatoes**
juice of 1 **lime**
3 cups **cooked basmati**
   or other **long-grain rice**,
   to serve

Heat the oil in a flameproof casserole or Dutch oven, add the onions, carrot, celery, bell peppers, and chile, and cook for 5 minutes. Add the paprika, cumin, and chopped stems of the cilantro, and cook for another 5 minutes, stirring occasionally, until the vegetables are softened. Add the turkey, beans, and tomatoes, mix well, and cover with a lid.

Transfer to a preheated oven, at 350°F, for 1½ hours, checking every 30 minutes and adding a little water if it starts to look dry.

Remove from the oven and stir in the lime juice and chopped cilantro leaves. Serve with the cooked rice.

For turkey & rice noodle stir-fry, cook 10 oz rice noodles according to the package directions. Heat 1 teaspoon sunflower oil in a wok and heat 3 cups cooked turkey strips for 2 minutes. Add 3 cups trimmed green beans, 1 sliced red onion, and 2 sliced garlic cloves and stir-fry for another 4–5 minutes. Stir in the juice of 1 lime, 1 teaspoon chili powder, 1 diced red chile, and 1 tablespoon gluten-free Thai fish sauce. Add 1 tablespoon chopped mint, 2 tablespoons chopped cilantro, and the drained rice noodles and toss well before serving. **Calories per serving 441**

chicken kiev

Calories per serving **489**
Serves **4**
Preparation time **20 minutes,
plus chilling**
Cooking time **40 minutes**

6 tablespoons **butter,**
softened
small handful of **parsley,**
finely chopped
6 **garlic cloves,** crushed
grated zest of 2 **lemons**
4 **boneless, skinless chicken
breasts** (about 5 oz each)
4 slices of **gluten-free bread**
3 tablespoons **gluten-free
all-purpose flour**
3 **eggs,** beaten
salt and **black pepper**
steamed **bok choy,** to serve

Mix together the butter, parsley, garlic, and lemon zest in a small bowl. Roll into 4 logs, then cover and put into the freezer for at least 30 minutes.

Slice the chicken breasts nearly in half horizontally. Open like a book, then place between 2 sheets of nonstick parchment paper or plastic wrap and flatten with a rolling pin or mallet. Place 1 garlic butter log in the center of each breast, then wrap the breasts around the butter, securing as tightly as possible with toothpicks.

Process the bread in a food processor to form bread crumbs, then transfer to a shallow bowl. Place the flour on a plate and season. Dip the rolled chicken breasts in the seasoned flour, then the beaten egg, and finally the bread crumbs until well coated. Roll again in the egg and crumbs, if necessary.

Transfer the kievs to a baking sheet and put into a preheated oven, at 400°F, for 40 minutes, until the chicken is golden and cooked through. Serve with steamed bok choy.

nutty stuffed flounder packages

Calories per serving **437**
Serves **4**
Preparation time **15 minutes**
Cooking time **20 minutes**

2 tablespoons **canola oil**
1¼ cups chopped **cremini
    mushrooms**
⅔ cup **roasted hazelnuts**,
    chopped
1½ teaspoons chopped
    parsley
4 **flounder fillets**, skinned
¼ cup **white wine**
2 tablespoons **butter**, cut
    into 4 pieces
13 oz **new potatoes**, halved
4 **Bibb**, **Boston**, or other
    small **butterhead lettuce**,
    quartered
1 tablespoon chopped **mint**
black pepper

Heat 1 tablespoon of the oil in a skillet, add the mushrooms, and cook for 5 minutes, until softened. Stir in the hazelnuts, then remove from the heat and stir in the parsley.

Lay the flounder fillets on a clean surface and divide the mushroom mixture among them, then roll up to enclose the stuffing. Place each fillet on a piece of aluminum foil large enough to enclose it, sprinkle with the white wine, season with black pepper, add 1 piece of the butter, and seal well. Bake in a preheated oven, at 400°F, for 15 minutes, or until cooked through.

Meanwhile, cook the potatoes in a saucepan of boiling water for 12–15 minutes, until tender. Heat the remaining oil in a skillet, add the lettuce, and sauté for 2–3 minutes on each side.

Drain the potatoes and season, then add the mint and lightly crush with a fork. Top with the flounder packages and serve with the lettuce.

For flounder & mushrooms with hazelnut broccoli,

put 4 flounder fillets in an ovenproof dish and cover with 3 cups sliced mushrooms. Sprinkle with the juice of 1 lemon and season. Dot with 2 tablespoons butter and bake in a preheated oven, at 350°F, for 16–17 minutes, basting frequently. Pour in ⅔ cup light cream and brown under a preheated hot broiler. Meanwhile, cook 11½ oz baby broccoli in a steamer for 3–4 minutes, until tender. Toss together with 2 tablespoons olive oil and 3 tablespoons chopped hazelnuts. Serve with the flounder. **Calories per serving 409**

sea bass with spinach dhal

Calories per serving **438**
Serves **4**
Preparation time **5 minutes**
Cooking time **30 minutes**

1½ tablespoons **olive oil**
1 **onion**, finely diced
2 **garlic cloves**, finely chopped
1 **green chile**, seeded and
   finely chopped
1 teaspoon **mustard seeds**
1 teaspoon **cumin seeds**
2 teaspoons **garam masala**
1 cup **red lentils**
1⅔ cups canned **diced
   tomatoes**
2½ cups **gluten-free
   vegetable broth**
4 **sea bass fillets** (about
   5 oz each)
7½ cups **spinach**
handful of **cilantro leaves**,
   chopped
salt and **black pepper**
1 tablespoon **toasted slivered
   almonds**, to garnish

Heat 1 tablespoon of the oil in a saucepan, add the onion, and sauté for 5 minutes, until soft. Stir in the garlic and chile and cook for another 1 minute. Add the seeds and garam masala and continue to cook for 2 minutes.

Stir in the lentils, tomatoes, and broth and bring to a boil. Reduce the heat and simmer for 20 minutes.

Meanwhile, heat the remaining oil in a separate large skillet and cook the sea bass for 3–4 minutes on each side, until cooked through.

Stir the spinach and chopped cilantro through the lentils until just starting to wilt, then season. Divide the dhal among 4 plates and top each one with a sea bass fillet. Serve sprinkled with toasted slivered almonds.

For broiled sea bass with garlicky spinach, cook 4 sea bass fillets (about 5 oz each) under a preheated hot broiler for 3–4 minutes on each side, until cooked through. Meanwhile, put 1¾ lb spinach into a saucepan and pour over a little boiling water, cover, and cook for 1–2 minutes, until the leaves start to wilt, then drain. Heat 1 tablespoon olive oil in a large skillet and cook 3 tablespoons pine nuts and 2 chopped garlic cloves for 2–3 minutes, then stir in the wilted spinach. Divide among 4 plates and top with the sea bass fillets.
Calories per serving 301

creamy shrimp curry

Calories per serving **482**
Serves **4**
Preparation time **5 minutes**
Cooking time **25–30 minutes**

1 tablespoon **sunflower oil**
1 **onion**, finely chopped
12 **curry leaves**
3 tablespoons **gluten-free curry paste**
1 cup **gluten-free fish broth**
2½ cups **coconut milk**
3 cups halved **green beans**
13 oz **peeled jumbo shrimp**
cilantro leaves, to garnish

Heat the oil in a wok or large skillet, add the onion, and sauté for 3–4 minutes, until soft. Add the curry leaves and cook for another 1 minute.

Stir in the curry paste and cook for 2 minutes, then pour in the broth and coconut milk and bring to a boil. Reduce the heat and simmer for 10–12 minutes.

Add the beans and cook for 5 minutes, until just tender, then add the shrimp and cook for another 3 minutes, until the shrimp turn pink and are cooked through. Serve sprinkled with a few cilantro leaves.

For spicy shrimp, heat 1 tablespoon olive oil in a skillet, add 3 peeled and chopped garlic cloves and 1 chopped red chile, and cook for 1 minute, then add 1 lb peeled jumbo shrimp and cook for 3–4 minutes, until the shrimp turn pink and are cooked through. Serve on a bed of crisp lettuce, sprinkled with the juice of 1 lime, black pepper, and a few cilantro leaves.
Calories per serving 135

bacon & leek tortilla

Calories per serving **483**
Serves **4**
Preparation time **10 minutes**
Cooking time **25–30 minutes**

4 tablespoons **olive oil**
2 **leeks**, trimmed, cleaned,
   and thickly sliced
11½ oz **new potatoes**, sliced
4 **lean bacon strips**, chopped
6 **extra-large eggs**
⅔ cup shredded **sharp
   cheddar cheese**
salt and **black pepper**

Heat the oil in a large flameproof skillet, add the leeks and potatoes, and sauté for 8–10 minutes, stirring frequently, until golden and tender. Add the bacon and cook for another 4–5 minutes, until cooked through.

Meanwhile, beat the eggs in a large bowl and add the cheese. Season well.

Stir the potato mixture into the beaten eggs, then return to the pan and cook over low heat for 8–10 minutes, making sure the bottom does not overcook.

Place the pan under a preheated hot broiler and cook for another 3–4 minutes, until the tortilla is cooked through and golden. Serve cut into wedges.

For leek, butternut & bacon soup, heat 2 tablespoons olive oil in a saucepan, add 3 trimmed, cleaned, and diced leeks and 3 cups peeled, seeded, and diced butternut squash, and cook for 3 minutes. Pour in 3¾ cups hot gluten-free vegetable broth and bring to a boil, then reduce the heat and simmer for 4–5 minutes, until the vegetables are soft. Meanwhile, cook 4 lean bacon strips under a preheated hot broiler until crisp, then coarsely chop. Stir 1¼ cups soy milk into the soup, then, using a handhand blender, blend the soup until smooth and season to taste. Ladle into 4 bowls and serve sprinkled with the bacon. **Calories per serving 249**

turkey balls with minty quinoa

Calories per serving **474**
Serves **4**
Preparation time **10 minutes,
  plus cooling**
Cooking time **25 minutes**

2 tablespoons **olive oil**
1 **onion**, finely chopped
1 **garlic clove**, crushed
1 **zucchini**, shredded
13 oz **ground turkey**
1 teaspoon **cumin seeds**
⅓ cup **feta cheese**
¼ cup chopped **parsley**
1½ cups **quinoa**
1⅓ cups **frozen peas**
⅓ cup chopped **mint**
grated zest and juice of
  1 **lemon**
3½ cups **arugula leaves**

Heat 1½ teaspoons of the oil in a skillet, add the onion and garlic, and sauté for 4–5 minutes, until softened, then let cool.

Mix together the cooked onion and garlic, zucchini, turkey, cumin seeds, feta, and half the parsley in a bowl. Shape into 12 balls and place on a baking sheet. Bake in a preheated oven, at 400°F, for 20 minutes, until cooked through.

Meanwhile, cook the quinoa in a saucepan of boiling water according to the package directions. In a separate pan of boiling water, cook the peas until tender. Drain the quinoa and peas, then transfer to a bowl and stir in the mint, remaining parsley, lemon zest and juice, and arugula leaves.

Serve the meatballs with the quinoa, drizzled with the remaining olive oil.

berry meringue desserts

Calories per serving **475**
Serves **6**
Preparation time **10 minutes,
    plus cooling**
Cooking time **1 hour**

3 **egg whites**
1¼ cups **superfine sugar**
1 teaspoon **white wine vinegar**
1¼ cups **heavy cream**
1⅔ cups **raspberries**, plus
    extra, left whole, to decorate
1⅓ cups hulled, quartered
    strawberries, plus extra,
    left whole and unhulled,
    to decorate
2 tablespoons **confectioners'
    sugar**
2 tablespoons **cream liqueur**

Line 2 large baking sheets with nonstick parchment paper.

Whisk the egg whites in a large, clean bowl until they form stiff peaks. Add the sugar, a spoonful at a time, and continue to whisk until thick and glossy. Fold in the vinegar with a large metal spoon.

Spoon or pipe 12 meringues onto the prepared baking sheets. Place in a preheated oven, at 300°F, for 1 hour, then turn off the oven and let the meringues cool completely. When cool, coarsely crush the meringues.

Whip the cream in a large bowl until it forms soft peaks. Coarsely crush together the raspberries and strawberries and stir into the cream. Fold in the crushed meringues, confectioners' sugar, and cream liqueur. Spoon into 6 tall glasses, decorate with extra berries, and serve immediately.

For mango & passion fruit meringue desserts, make the meringues as above and coarsely crush. Whip the cream with 2 tablespoons confectioners' sugar in a large bowl until it forms soft peaks. Peel and pit 1 large mango and puree half the flesh in a food processor or blender. Chop the remaining mango flesh and stir all the mango into the cream mixture with the scooped flesh of 2 passion fruit. Fold in the crushed meringues and serve immediately. **Calories per serving 482**

white chocolate risotto

Calories per serving **410**
Serves **6**
Preparation time **10 minutes**
Cooking time **25 minutes**

2 tablespoons **unsalted butter**
1 **vanilla bean**, split in half
    lengthwise
1 ⅓ cups **risotto rice**
¼ cup **superfine sugar**
⅓ cup **white wine**
3 cups **milk**
3 oz **gluten-free white
    chocolate**, grated
6 **peaches**, halved and pitted

Melt the butter in a heavy saucepan. Scrape in the seeds from the vanilla bean and cook, stirring, for a few minutes. Stir in the rice and 2 tablespoons of the sugar and mix well. Pour in the wine, bring to a boil, and cook, stirring constantly, until the liquid has been absorbed.

Add a little of the milk and gently simmer, stirring, until the milk has been absorbed. Continue to add the milk until the rice is soft but still holds its shape.

Remove the pan from the heat and stir in the grated chocolate, then cover and let stand.

Meanwhile, sprinkle the cut halves of the peaches with the remaining sugar and cook under a preheated broiler until golden and bubbling.

Spoon the risotto into 6 serving bowls and top each with 2 broiled peach halves.

For quick peach & rice dessert, divide 3¼ cups drained canned peaches in juice between 6 ramekins, then top with 1⅓ cups prepared rice pudding. Sprinkle each one with 1½ teaspoon Demerara or other raw sugar and cook under a preheated broiler until bubbling. Let cool before serving. **Calories per serving 157**

index

acknowledgments

Senior Commissioning Editor: Eleanor Maxfield
Project Editor: Clare Churly
Design and Art Direction: Geoff Fennell
Special Photography: William Shaw
Food Stylist: Joy Skipper
Prop Stylist: Liz Hippisley
Picture Library Manager: Jennifer Veall
Production Controller: Sarah Kramer

Special photography © Octopus Publishing Group Limited/William Shaw. **Additional photography** © Octopus Publishing Group Limited/Will Heap 67, 217; David Munns 105, 151, 155, 163; Sean Myers 41; Emma Neish 129, 143; Lis Parsons 11, 31, 75, 89, 99, 121, 147, 149, 167, 171, 187, 199, 205, 223, 229; William Reavell 211; William Shaw 25, 29, 33, 35, 37, 39, 43, 45, 51, 53, 59, 63, 73, 81, 83, 87, 93, 113, 123, 125, 133, 135, 141, 159, 173, 175, 179, 181, 189, 191, 233.